Corporate Manslau
Corporate Homicid

AUSTRALIA
Law Book Co.
Sydney

CANADA and USA
Carswell
Toronto

HONG KONG
Sweet & Maxwell Asia

NEW ZEALAND
Brookers
Wellington

SINGAPORE and MALAYSIA
Sweet & Maxwell Asia
Singapore and Kuala Lumpur

Corporate Manslaughter and Corporate Homicide Act 2007

Annotations
by

Peter Gray QC
Compass Chambers
Faculty of Advocates
Edinburgh

&

Rona Jamieson
Solicitor and Partner
Paull & Williamsons
Aberdeen

THOMSON

W. GREEN

Published in 2008 by
W. Green & Son Ltd
21 Alva Street
Edinburgh EH2 4PS

www.wgreen.thomson.com

Printed in Great Britain by Athenaeum Press Ltd, Gateshead

No natural forests were destroyed to make this product;
only farmed timber was used and replanted

A CIP catalogue record for this book is available from
the British Library.

ISBN 978-0-414-01696-5

CONTENTS

TABLE OF CASES

TABLE OF STATUTES

TABLE OF STATUTORY INSTRUMENTS

CORPORATE MANSLAUGHTER AND CORPORATE HOMICIDE ACT 2007

(2007 C19)

CONTENTS

Corporate Manslaughter and Corporate Homicide Act 2007

An Act to create a new offence that, in England and Wales or Northern Ireland, is to be called corporate manslaughter and, in Scotland, is to be called corporate homicide; and to make provision in connection with that offence.

[26th July 2007]

Corporate Manslaughter and Corporate Homicide

The offence

1.01 **1.**—(1) An organisation to which this section applies is guilty of an offence if the way in which its activities are managed or organised—

(a) causes a person's death, and

(b) amounts to a gross breach of a relevant duty of care owed by the organisation to the deceased.

(2) The organisations to which this section applies are—

(a) a corporation;

(b) a department or other body listed in Schedule 1;

(c) a police force;

(d) a partnership, or trade union or employers' association, that is an employer.

(3) An organisation is guilty of an offence under this section only if the way in which its activities are managed or organised by its senior management is a substantial element in the breach referred to in subsection (1).

(4) For the purposes of this Act —

(a) "relevant duty of care" has the meaning given by section 2, read with sections 3 to 7;

(b) a breach of duty of care by an organisation is a "gross" breach if the conduct alleged to amount to a breach of that duty falls far below what can reasonably be expected of the organisation in the circumstances;

(c) "senior management", in relation to an organisation, means the persons who play significant roles in—

(i) the making of decisions about how the whole or a substantial part of its activities are to be managed or organised, or

(ii) the actual managing or organising of the whole or a substantial part of those activities.

(5) The offence under this section is called—

(a) corporate manslaughter, in so far as it is an offence under the law of England and Wales or Northern Ireland;

(b) corporate homicide, in so far as it is an offence under the law of Scotland.

(6) An organisation that is guilty of corporate manslaughter or corporate homicide is liable on conviction on indictment to a fine.

(7) The offence or corporate homicide is indictable only in the High Court of Justiciary.

DEFINITIONS

1.02 "corporation": s.25

"gross breach": s.1(4)(b)

"partnership": s.25

"police force": s.13(1)

"relevant duty of care": s.1(4)(a) and ss.2–7

"senior management": s.1(4)(c)

"trade union": s.25

The offence

GENERAL NOTE

Subsection (1) "managed or organised"   **1.03**

This phrasing comes direct from the English Law Commission Report of 1996, *Legislating the Criminal Code, Involuntary Manslaughter* (Law Com. No.237; see Appendix 2, extract of No.237, Pt VIII, *A New Offence of Corporate Killing*). It is not intended that an organisation be liable automatically for the negligence of an employee. The Law Commission recommended that the offence should apply only in cases where "the conduct in question amounted to a failure to ensure safety in the management or organisation of the corporation's activities". In each case it would be a question for the jury to determine whether the conduct amounted to such "management failure" or "operational negligence"—the former being conduct of the corporation for which it would be directly liable and the latter being conduct of its employees for which it would not be liable (Law Com. No.237, paras 8.8–8.34). Similar considerations may apply in determining whether a failure is due to management or organisation functions as would be applied in determining whether an individual was a controlling mind under the old common law principle (*Tesco Supermarkets v Nattrass* [1972] A.C. 153). It is the nature of the conduct which is relevant, rather than the status of the individual responsible (Law Com. No.237, para.8.8). This includes failures in the provision of safe systems of work, equipment, premises and competent workers. The Law Commission proposed that such duties be extended to "all those who might be affected by" an organisation's activities but the government has chosen to limit the duty to the particular categories set out in s.2.

The following cases cited by the English Law Commission in its analysis of management failure (Law Com. No.237, paras 8.24–8.35) provide examples of conduct which would be likely to be regarded as failures in the management or organisation of activities for the purposes of s.1 of the Act:

- *Sword v Cameron* (1839) 1 D. 493 (defective system of work)
- *Wilson and Clyde Coal Co. v English* [1938] A.C. 57 (HL) (unsafe system)
- *Smith v Baker & Sons* [1891] A.C. 325 (HL) (work equipment)
- *Speed v Swift (Thomas) & Co Ltd* [1943] 1 K.B. 557 (failure to adapt system to special circumstance)
- *General Cleaning Contractors Ltd v Christmas* [1953] A.C. 180 (precautions left to employee's initiative)
- *Rees v Cumbrian Wagon Works Ltd* (1946) 175 L.T. 220 (CA) (supervision failure)
- *McDermid v Nash Dredging & Reclaiming Co. Ltd* [1987] A.C. 906 (3rd party failed to provide safe system)

By contrast it is arguable that the following examples of "operational negligence", as opposed to "management failure", would be unlikely to give rise to liability under the Act:

- *Colfar v Coggins & Griffiths (Liverpool) Ltd* [1945] A.C. 197 (HL) (casual act of negligence by fellow worker)
- *Winter v Cardiff Rural District Council* [1950] 1 All E.R. 819 (routine task)

Subsection (1)(a) Causation   **1.04**

Ordinary principles of causation apply in determining whether the way in which the organisation's activities were managed or organised caused the death.

It is not necessary for the management failure to have been the sole or even the principal cause of death. It will be sufficient for the prosecution to establish a causal connection which is not merely *de minimis* (*Watson v HMA*, 1978 S.C.C.R. (Supp.) 192; *R v Shelton*, 1995 R.T.R. 635).

The jury requires to be satisfied beyond reasonable doubt that the death would not have occurred had it not been for the management failure. The management failure requires to be a cause, but not necessarily the immediate cause, which will normally be some act or omission of "operational negligence". The management failure lies in failing to anticipate the foreseeable act of operational negligence and creating systems to prevent its occurrence (see Law Com. No.237, paras 8.36–8.37).

The issue of causation is likely to be contentious in the vast majority of prosecutions brought under the Act. If an organisation's failure to prevent a single act of carelessness through lack of supervision is sufficient causation, almost every act of operational negligence would be capable of being deemed to have been caused, to some extent, by a management failure, on the basis that a supervisor's presence would probably have prevented it. That is at odds with the view that not every act of operational negligence should amount to management failure. The Law Commission rejected a strict liability approach where every act of operational negligence was automatically attributed to the organisation (Law Com. No.237, para.8.18). They favoured the

3

distinction drawn in *Wilson and Clyde Coal co Ltd v English*, 1936 S.C. 883, between failures which are permanent or continuous and those which arise from casual acts emerging in the course of a day's work.

Notwithstanding that, one of the commission's recommendations was that the Act contain an express provision to the effect that management failure may be regarded as a cause of death, even if the immediate cause is the act or omission of an individual. Arguably that would have prevented the chain ever being broken by an act of negligence (as opposed to deliberate harm). That recommendation was not adopted and there is no such provision in the Act. It would therefore appear open to the defence to argue in any case involving clear operational negligence by an individual employee that the chain of causation has been broken. It will be a matter for the jury to consider in each case.

It is foreseeable, for example, that individual workers will from time to time be careless and make mistakes and in those circumstances an organisation is required to develop systems to guard against human fallibility. Where an employee deliberately chooses not to follow a work instruction or safe working method, or behaves in a grossly negligent manner, it may be an intervening act which breaks the chain of causation. The reason for the employee's failure will require to be examined. If the specified system of work was cumbersome, or the reasons for it were not well understood, or it had become custom and practice to follow an alternative method, it is unlikely that the employee's act would break the chain of causation between the management failure and the death.

1.05 *Subsection (2)(a) Corporations*

"Corporation" does not include a corporation sole but includes any body corporate wherever incorporated (s.25).

A holding company may be liable for a death provided it owed a duty of care to the deceased and there were failings in the management of the holding company which amounted to a gross breach (see debate, *Hansard*, HL, col.GC166 (January 11, 2007)). A parent company, however, would not be held vicariously liable for failings of the subsidiary (Ministry of Justice, *A Guide to the Corporate Manslaughter and Corporate Homicide Act 2007*, p.6).

The offence applies to foreign companies if operating in the UK. Where a company is incorporated in a foreign jurisdiction and operating through a UK subsidiary, the subsidiary would be likely to face investigation and prosecution (*Guide to the Corporate Manslaughter and Corporate Homicide Act*, p.6).

1.06 *Subsection (2)(d)*

This section was added by Lords' amendment. It brings partnerships, trade unions and employers' associations within the scope of the offence, if they are themselves employers. The offence can be extended to other types of unincorporated organisations but requires an affirmative resolution of both Houses (see s.24).

1.07 *Subsection (3) Senior Management Failure*

The original government proposals for the Bill (Cm. 6497) required senior management failure to be an essential element of the offence. The Home Affairs and Work Pensions Committees ("the HAWPC") suggested that the requirement that senior management failure be "essential" could encourage organisations to reduce the priority given to health and safety (para.136) and lead to legal argument over who was and who was not a "senior manager" (para.149) (see House of Commons Home Affairs and Work and Pensions Committees, First Joint Report of Session 2005–06, HC 540). Following consideration of the proposals by the HAWPC, the Government accepted that the test should be reconsidered (Cm. 6755, p.15) and this was reflected in the Bill as presented to Parliament in July 2006 (Bill 220/2006).

The offence, as defined in the Act, removes the requirement that senior management failure be an "essential" element but requires it to be a "substantial" element. Potentially, this may lead to legal argument over not only the meaning of "senior management" but also the meaning of "substantial element". It is a question of fact to be determined by the jury in the circumstances of each case.

1.08 *Subsection (4)(b) Gross Breach*

The Government's intention is that the offence requires the same degree of negligence as the English common law offence of gross negligence manslaughter. The definition of gross negligence, as conduct that "falls far below what can reasonably be expected of the organisation in the circumstances" is adopted from the Law Commission Report (No.237).

"Far below" is not defined and has been criticised for introducing uncertainty (see *Hansard*, HL, cols GC140–146 (January 11, 2007)).

The Law Commission took the view that industry practice should be relevant in determining whether in any particular case an organisation has met the standards to be "reasonably expected of an organisation in the circumstances". In its view, failure to comply with established industry practice is likely to be seen as falling "far below"; on the other hand the mere fact that a particular practice is common in an industry does not necessarily mean that it cannot be regarded as falling "far below" what can be reasonably expected (Law Com. No.237, para.8.7).

The Ministry of Justice, in its guide, suggest that factors which may be taken into account include the systems of work used, the level of training provided and adequacy of equipment, issues of immediate supervision and middle management, the organisation's strategic approach to health and safety and its arrangements for assessing risks and monitoring and auditing its processes (*Guide to the Corporate Manslaughter and Corporate Homicide Act*, p.12).

The jury is entitled to consider not only the organisation's formal management systems, but broader attitudes within the organisation towards safety (*Guide to the Corporate Manslaughter and Corporate Homicide Act*, p.13).

The government's intention is that the corporate offence should apply in similar circumstances to those in which individuals would be held responsible for killing by gross negligence, a concept which is familiar in English criminal law.

The test for gross negligence manslaughter in English law does not require "recklessness", as is explained in the House of Lords' decision in *R v Adomako* [1995] 1 A.C. 171. In that case an anaesthetist was assisting at an eye operation. A tube became disconnected from a ventilator causing the patient to suffer a cardiac arrest and die. The anaesthetist was convicted of involuntary manslaughter and appealed on the basis it was insufficient to direct the jury in relation to the gross negligence test without reference to the test of recklessness.

During the trial it was conceded that, whilst the conduct of the anaesthetist had been negligent, the issue was whether his conduct was criminal.

The House of Lords held (Lord Mackay of Clashfern LC) that:

> "[T]he ordinary principles of the law of negligence apply to ascertain whether or not the defendant has been in breach of a duty of care towards the victim who has died. If such breach of duty is established, the next question is whether that breach of duty caused the death of the victim. If so, the jury must go on to consider whether that breach of duty should be characterised as gross negligence and therefore a crime. This will depend on the seriousness of the breach of duty committed by the defendant in all the circumstances in which the defendant was placed when it occurred. The jury will have to consider the extent to which the defendant's conduct departed from the standard of care incumbent upon him, involving as it must have done, a risk of death to the patient, was such that it should be judged criminal." (*R v Adomako* [1995] 1 A.C. 171, p.187.)

In response to criticism that this involved circularity, because the jury must decide whether the negligence was criminal in order for a crime to be committed, Lord MacKay explained:

> "It is true that to a certain extent this involves an element of circularity but in this branch of the law, I do not believe that is fatal to it being correct as a test of how far conduct must depart from excepted standards to be characterised as criminal. This is necessarily a question of degree and an attempt to specify that degree more closely is, I think, likely to achieve only a spurious precision. The essence of the matter which is supremely a jury question is whether having regard to the risk of death involved, the conduct of the defendant was so bad in all the circumstances as to amount in their judgement to a criminal act or omission." (*R v Adomako*, p.187.)

Lord Mackay took the view that it was appropriate to use the word "reckless", but in the ordinary meaning of that word, without giving detailed directions to the jury with regard to the legal meaning of the term. He went on to say:

> "While ... I have said in my view it is perfectly open to a trial judge to use the word 'reckless' if it appears appropriate in the circumstances of a particular case as indicating the extent to which a defendant's conduct must deviate from that of a proper standard of

care, I do not think it right to require that this should be done and certainly not right that it should incorporate the full detail required in *Lawrence*."[1] (*R v Adomako*, p.189.)

The test as outlined in *Adomako* has been criticised as too uncertain. In *R v Misra and Srivastava* [2005] 1 Cr. App. R.21; [2004] EWCA Crim. 2375 the test was challenged (unsuccessfully) on the basis that the uncertainty was such that the test was contrary to the provisions of the Human Rights Act 1998.

The Court of Appeal rejected that submission. It considered the case of *Adomako* and *R v Singh* [1999] Crim. L.R. 582. In that case, the court approved the trial judge's direction in a case of manslaughter by gross negligence, that "the circumstances must be such that a reasonably prudent person would have foreseen a serious and obvious risk not merely of injury, even serious injury but of death". The court stated:

> "In our judgement, where the issue of risk is engaged, *Adomako* demonstrates, and it is now clearly established, that it relates to the risk of death and is not sufficiently satisfied by the risk of bodily injury or injury to health. In short, the offence requires gross negligence in circumstances where what is at risk is the life of an individual to whom the defendant owes a duty of care." (*R v Singh* [2005] 1 Cr. App. R. 21, para.52.)

The court held that the jury is not being asked to consider whether or not conduct amounts to a crime but rather:

> " 'The jury must go on to consider whether that breach of duty should be characterised as gross negligence and *therefore* as a crime.' ... On proper analysis, therefore, the jury is not deciding whether the particular defendant ought to be convicted on some unprincipled basis. The question for the jury is not whether the defendant's conduct was gross and whether additionally it was a crime but whether his behaviour was grossly negligence and consequently criminal ...
> 64. In our judgement, the law is clear. The ingredients of the offence have been clearly defined, and the principles decided in the House of Lords in *Adomako*. They involve no uncertainty. The hypothetical citizen seeking to know his position should be advised that, assuming he owed a duty of care to the deceased which he had negligently broken, and that death resulted, he would be liable to conviction for manslaughter, if on the available evidence the jury was satisfied that his negligence was gross. A doctor would be told that grossly negligent treatment of a patient which exposed him or her to the risk of death, and caused it, would constitute manslaughter." (*R v Singh* [2005] 1 Cr. App. R. 21, paras 62 and 64.)

Notwithstanding the decision in *Misra* (above), s.8 of the Act contains "guidance to the jury on factors to consider when assessing" whether conduct amounts to gross breach in an attempt to address this criticism (see para.8.01).

1.10 *Foreseeability*

One of the key elements of the offence of killing by gross carelessness under English common law is the requirement that the risk of death, as opposed to simply injury, be obvious to any reasonable person in that position (Law Com. Rep, no.237, para.8.2; *R v Singh* [1999] Crim. L.R. 582).

The Law Commission recommended that there be no similar requirement in relation to corporate manslaughter, a recommendation which appears to have been accepted (Law Com. No.237, para.8.4).

1.11 *Subsection (1)(4)(c) Senior Management*

In determining what amounts to a "substantial part" of an organisation's activities, the scale of the activities overall should be considered. It is intended to include, for example, regional and divisional managers. The levels of management covered will depend on the size of the organisation as a whole; it is suggested that the manager of a single retail outlet may be included if

---

[1] This is a reference to the case of *R v Lawrence (Stephen)* [1982] A.C. 510 where the test of recklessness was propounded and which stated that to convict for involuntary manslaughter there must be recklessness or wilful knowledge of risk which might bring about serious injury or death.

employed by a small organisation, but may be deemed to have an insufficiently "senior" management role if employed by a larger national chain (Cm. 6497, para.30). The authors of the guide published by the Ministry of Justice regard senior management as those who make significant decisions about the organisation, or substantial parts of it. It is not limited to those in operational positions but includes those carrying out financial or strategic roles or having some central responsibility for health and safety (*Guide to the Corporate Manslaughter and Corporate Homicide Act*, p.13). In addition to directors and similar officers, roles likely to be regarded as senior management will include regional and divisional managers, although the issue will depend on the nature and scale of each organisation's activities (*Guide to the Corporate Manslaughter and Corporate Homicide Act*, p.13).

It was argued that the requirement for senior management involvement in the offence would encourage inappropriate delegation of responsibility for health and safety management to a junior level. Such concerns were dismissed by the government during the lengthy House of Lords debate on the Bill on the basis that appropriate delegation and appropriate supervision of such delegation is part of the proper management of health and safety. They argued that delegating responsibility out of the boardroom entirely is unlikely ever to be seen by the courts as appropriate (see *Hansard*, HL, col.GC135 (January 11, 2007)).

Subsection (6) Fine **1.12**

The sanction for breach of the offence is a fine. There is no limit to the level of fine which may be imposed. In the context of offences under the Health and Safety at Work etc. Act 1974 ("the HSWA"), much assistance has been provided in relation to establishing factors which may be relevant to sentence by a number of English sentencing guideline cases, and in particular *R v Howe & Son (Engineers) Ltd* [1999] All E.R. 249, *R v Friskies Petcare Ltd* (2002) Cr. App. R.(S.) 201, *R v Colthrop Board Mills* (2002) 2 Cr. App. R.(S.) 80 and *R v Jarvis Facilities Ltd* (2005) All E.R. (D.) 429. These cases are likely to continue to be of assistance when attempting to identify aggravating or mitigating features in cases brought under the Corporate Manslaughter and Corporate Homicide Act ("the CMCHA"). However, what is not known is how level of fines imposed in respect of a conviction under CMCHA will compare with fines imposed in respect of a conviction under s.2 or s.3 of the HSWA. However, the issue of sentencing generally in relation to the new Act is a matter upon which the Sentencing Advisory Panel ("the SAP") in England has been asked by the Sentencing Guidelines Council to advise. The panel published a consultation paper in November 2007, in which it stated that:

> "[T]he Panel is consulting on sentencing for both corporate manslaughter and breaches of health and safety law that result in death, in order to promote consistency and to produce guidelines that properly reflect the seriousness of the offending involved." (Sentencing Advisory Panel, *Consultation Paper on Sentencing for Corporate Manslaughter*, November 15, 2007; see Appendix 4.)

In relation to the approach to be taken in assessing the appropriate level of financial penalty for offences under each Act, the panel has expressed the following views:

> "58. The Panel's provisional view is that annual turnover is the most appropriate measure of an organisation's ability to pay a fine, and thus the starting points and ranges proposed below are expressed as percentages of annual turnover. It would be for the prosecution to provide evidence of particularly high profitability if it considered the fine indicated by annual turnover to be too low, or for the offender to provide evidence of low liquidity if it considered the fine indicated by annual turnover to be too high.
>
> 59. The statutory offence of corporate manslaughter has been created for the most serious instances of management failure resulting in death. The Panel's view is that a fine imposed for an offence under the CMA should be set at a level significantly higher than for an offence under the HSWA involving death. The fine levels proposed below for offences of corporate manslaughter are based on the assumption that a publicity order will be imposed on the offender.
>
> 60. The Panel's provisional starting point for an offence of corporate manslaughter committed by a first time offender pleading not guilty is a fine amounting to 5 per cent of the offender's average annual turnover during the three years prior to sentencing .... The court will then take into account any aggravating and/or mitigating factors as set out above, arriving at a fine which will normally fall within a range of 2.5 to 10 per cent of average annual turnover. Significant aggravating factors or previous convictions may take

the fine beyond the range. The court will then consider any mitigation related to the offender (rather than the offence), which may take the fine below the range.

61. The Panel's provisional starting point for an offence under the HSWA involving death is a fine amounting to 2.5 per cent of average annual turnover during the three years prior to the offence. The fine will normally fall within a range of 1 to 7.5 per cent of average annual turnover.

62. Where the offender is a very large organisation, the Panel's provisional approach would result in larger fines than have been imposed previously by the courts. The largest fine imposed to date for a health and safety offence in the UK was that of £15 million in the Scottish case of Transco, for breaches of regulations which led to the deaths of four members of the same family in a gas explosion. The fine represented 5 per cent of the company's after-tax profits and less than one per cent of annual turnover. Although in that instance the offender did respond appropriately to the incident, it has been suggested that the fine in itself could be easily absorbed and may not have provided an effective individual or general deterrent as described above. A fine expressed as a percentage of average annual turnover is designed to have an equal economic impact on all sizes of organisation, in order to reflect the seriousness of the offence even where the offender has large financial resources.

63. Conversely, where the offender has a very low annual turnover, it is possible that the Panel's provisional approach would result in smaller fines than those currently imposed in some cases, at least for offences under the HSWA resulting in death. The apparent disparity in actual terms between fines imposed on very small and very large offenders is an inevitable result of an approach designed to have a consistently equal economic impact. However, it may be thought appropriate to set a minimum fine for corporate manslaughter or for offences under the HSWA involving death, in order to ensure that the harm involved in such offences is properly reflected in the sentence.

...

74. In summary, the assessment of financial circumstances will seek to ensure that:
  (a) the fine is sufficient to have the required impact, in most cases without imperilling either the existence of the organisation or the funds necessary to remedy defective systems; and
  (b) where the offender is funded from the public purse, it is recognised that the fine will be paid with public money.
  ...

90. When sentencing for an offence of corporate manslaughter, the starting point should be:
  • the imposition of a publicity order ... ; and
  • a fine of 5 per cent of the offender's average annual turnover (see para.60);
  • within a fine range of 2.5–10 per cent of average annual turnover.

91. When sentencing for an offence under the HSWA involving death, the starting point should be:
  • a fine of 2.5 per cent of the offender's average annual turnover (see para.61);
  • within a fine range of 1–7.5 per cent of average annual turnover."

It is understood that the Sentencing Guidelines Council will finalise its position by the autumn of 2008.

Reaction to the SAP consultation paper has been mixed. In response to the SAP guidelines on how courts should sentence organisations convicted of manslaughter, David Bergman, Executive Director of the Centre for Corporate Accountability ("the CCA"), stated:

"These proposals need to be given significant consideration. However, in light of the seriousness of the criminal offence of corporate manslaughter, our initial response is that the proposed levels of fines are simply too low. Fines of between 2.5 to 10 percent of the annual turnover of an organisation convicted of manslaughter are too low... Organisations convicted of killing people should face the threat of far larger fines than those organisations who are found to have been involved in breaking European competition law—which currently attracts a maximum 'administrative' fine of 10 per cent of the annual global turnover of the organisation." (CCA press release, *Proposed Fines for Corporate Manslaughter conviction inadequate says safety charity*, November 21, 2007.)

By contrast, the Confederation of British Industry ("the CBI") said many of its members felt "considerable concern" over proposals to fine companies up to a tenth of their global turnover for offences under the manslaughter law passed this year. Janet Asherson, head of Health and Safety at the CBI, said many members had criticised the panel's plan to fine companies between 2.5 and 10 per cent of annual turnover, which could equate to hundreds of millions of pounds for large multinationals. She said, "[t]here is considerable concern both at the CBI and among our businesses that the crude use of this figure could be way out of proportion".

Subsection (7) Indictable only in High Court **1.13**
   In Scotland, as with common law culpable homicide, the offence requires to be prosecuted on indictment in the High Court of Justiciary.

Relevant duty of care

Meaning of "relevant duty of care"

   2.—(1) A "relevant duty of care", in relation to an organisation, means **2.01**
any of the following duties owed by it under the law of negligence—
   (a) a duty owed to its employees or to other persons working for the organisation or performing services for it;
   (b) a duty owed as occupier of premises;
   (c) a duty owed in connection with—
      (i) the supply by the organisation of goods or services (whether for consideration or not),
      (ii) the carrying on by the organisation of any construction or maintenance operations,
      (iii) the carrying on by the organisation of any other activity on a commercial basis, or
         the use or keeping by the organisation of any plant, vehicle or other thing.
   (d) A duty owed to a person who, by reason of being a person within subsection (2) is someone for whose safety the organisation is responsible.
   (2) A person is within this subsection if—
   (a) he is detained at a custodial institution or in a custody area at a court or police station;
   (b) he is detained at a removal centre or short-term holding facility;
   (c) he is being transported in a vehicle, or being held in any premises, in pursuance of prison escort arrangements or immigration escort arrangements;
   (d) he is living in secure accommodation in which he has been placed;
   (e) he is a detained patient.
   (3) Subsection (1) is subject to sections 3 to 7.
   (4) A reference in subsection (1) to a duty owed under the law of negligence includes a reference to a duty that would be owed under the law of negligence but for any statutory provision under which liability is imposed in place of liability under that law.
   (5) For the purposes of this Act, whether a particular organisation owes a duty of care to a particular individual is a question of law.
   The Judge must make any findings of fact necessary to decide that question.
   (6) For the purposes of this Act there is to be disregarded—
   (a) any rule of the common law that has the effect of preventing a duty of care from being owed by one person to another by reason of the fact that they are jointly engaged in unlawful conduct;
   (b) Any such rule that has the effect of preventing a duty of care from being owed to a person by reason of his acceptance of a risk of harm.
   (7) In this section—

"construction or maintenance operations" means operations of any of the
following descriptions—
  (a) construction, installation, alteration, extension, improvement,
      repair, maintenance, decoration, cleaning, demolition or dis-
      mantling of—
        (i) any building or structure,
        (ii) anything else that forms, or is to form, part of the land, or
        (iii) any plant, vehicle or other thing;
  (b) operations that form an integral part of, or are preparatory to,
      or are for rendering complete, any operations within paragraph
      (a);
"custodial institution" means a prison, a young offender institution, a
    secure training centre, a young offenders institution, a young offen-
    ders centre, a juvenile justice centre or a remand centre;
"detained patient" means—
  (a) a person who is detained in any premises under—
        (i) Part 2 or 3 of the Mental Health Act 1983 (c.20) ("the
            1983 Act"), or
        (ii) Part 2 or 3 of the Mental Health (Northern Ireland)
             Order 1986 (S.I. 1986/595 (N.I. 4)) ("the 1986 Order");
  (b) a person who (otherwise than by reason of being detained as
      mentioned in paragraph (a)) is deemed to be in legal custody by
        (i) section 137 of 1983 Act
        (ii) Article 131 of the 1986 Order, or
        (iii) Article 11 of the Mental Health (Care and Treatment)
              (Scotland) Act 2003 (Consequential Provisions) Order
              2005 (S.I. 2005/2078);
  (c) a person who is detained in any premises, or is otherwise in
      custody, under the Mental Health (Care and Treatment)
      (Scotland) Act 2003 (asp 13) or Part 6 of the Criminal Proce-
      dure (Scotland) Act 1995 (c.46) or who is detained in a hospital
      under section 200 of that Act of 1995;
"immigration escort arrangements" means arrangements made under
    section 156 of the Immigration and Asylum Act 1999(c.33);
"the law of negligence" includes—
  (a) in relation to England and Wales, the Occupiers' Liability act
      1957 (c.31), the Defective Premises Act 1972 (c.35) and the
      Occupiers' Liability Act 1984 (c.3);
  (b) in relation to Scotland, the Occupiers' Liability (Scotland) Act
      1960 (c.30);
  (c) in relation to Northern Ireland, the Occupiers' Liability Act
      (Northern Ireland) 1957 (c.25), the Defective Premises
      (Northern Ireland) Order 1975 (S.I. 1975/1039 (N.I.9)), the
      Occupiers' Liability (Northern Ireland) Order 1987 (S.I. 1987/
      1280 (N.I.15)) and the Defective Premises (Landlord's Liabi-
      lity) Act (Northern Ireland) 2001 (c.10);
"prison escort arrangements" means arrangements made under section 80
    of the Criminal Justice Act 1991 (c.53) or under section 102 or 118 of
    the Criminal Justice and Public Order Act 1994 (c.33);
"removal centre" and "short-term holding facility" have the meaning
    given by section 147 of the Immigration and Asylum Act 1999;
"secure accommodation" means accommodation, not consisting of or
    forming part of a custodial institution, provided for the purpose of
    restricting the liberty of persons under the age of 18.

DEFINITIONS

"Employee" is defined in s.25: means an individual who works under a contract of employment or apprenticeship (whether express or implied and, if express, whether oral or in writing) and related expressions are to be construed accordingly. **2.02**

GENERAL NOTE

The requirement for a duty of care is well understood in relation to delictual claims but is new to Scots criminal law. It is testament to the Act's English roots, in the English common law offence of gross negligence manslaughter.[2] The government's intention is that the statutory offence should apply only in circumstances where organisations were already subject to gross negligence manslaughter at common law (Cm. 6497). **2.03**

Subsection (1) **2.04**

For the new offence to apply the organisation must have owed a "relevant duty of care" to the deceased.

For a detailed review of the concept of duty of care see: William J. Stewart, *Reparation: Liability for Delict*, Chs 11–27.

The Act identifies the types of relationship which will give rise to a relevant duty of care for the purposes of the new offence. Where such relationships are well recognised as giving rise to a duty of care in law there is no need, as Stewart puts it, to reinvent the wheel. Where "a person is run down by a snow mobile or a jet ski rather than a motor car" the basic duty is the same. "The only difference is that it will be harder to say that the duty was breached—what particular things should have been done by the jet skier" without the benefit of a clear line of precedent.

That neatly sums up the problem in determining the scope of the duties in s.2(1)(a)–(d).

Subsection (2) **2.05**

(a) Employers Liability **2.05.1**

It is well established both under the common law and various statutory provisions that a duty of care exists between an employer and employee. The extent of the duty in relation to other persons working for the organisation or performing services for it is less clear. In common law the duty is owed only to an employee (however, see *Nelhams v Sandells Maintenance Ltd & Gillespie (UK) Ltd* [1996] P.I.Q.R. P.52; Stewart, Ch.20, s.A20–013). The Management of Health & Safety at Work Regulations 1999 creates duties in relation to workers other than employees but a civil right of action for breach of the duty is limited only to employees (reg.22).

(b) Occupiers Liability **2.05.2**

The Occupiers Liability (Scotland) Act 1960 provides that an occupier of premises owes a duty of care to those entering the premises, in respect of any dangers due to the state of the premises or anything done or omitted to be done on them. The Act does not draw a distinction between different categories of person entering on premises, although the steps required to comply with the duty may vary from case to case. Those entering premises unexpectedly, such as firemen are owed a duty (Stewart, Ch.19, s.A19–004) and those trespassing or otherwise entering without permission (see *Dawson v Scottish Power*, 1999 S.L.T. 672).

The occupier of premises is the person "occupying or having control of land or other premises" (s.1(1)). A landlord with responsibility for maintenance or repair of premises owes similar duties, even if not in physical occupation (s.3(1)). Dangers due to the state of the premises includes dangers due to things left on the premises and is not restricted to the subjects themselves (*Dunn v Carlin*, 2003 G.W.D. 5–130, where petrol was left exposed and subsequently ignited). See also *Hill v Lovett*, 1992 S.L.T. 994 in relation to animals kept on premises.

(c)   *(i) Supply of Goods or Services.* See Stewart, Ch.21, s.A21–002 and *Donaghue v Stevenson*, **2.05.3** 1932 S.C. (H.L.) 31. A manufacturer of products "owes a duty to the consumer" to take reasonable care (*Donaghue v Stevenson*, p.57).

(ii) Construction or Maintenance Operations. "Construction or Maintenance Operations" is given a wide meaning (see subs.(7) above). In addition to duties owed as employers or occupiers, those carrying on construction or maintenance operations may owe duties of care to those carrying out construction work under their control.

(iii) Any Other Commercial Activity. This appears to be a "catch all" provision in the

---

[2]   See *R v Adomako* [1995] 1 A.C. 79 and general commentary on s.1.

event that there are circumstances where an organisation owes a duty of care in circumstances where the activity is not covered by any of the other categories. "Commercial basis" is not defined. The provision is intended to apply to activities such as farming or mining (Bill 5, Explanatory Notes, para.21).

(iv) The Use or Keeping of Any Plants, Vehicle or Other Thing. This appears to be a further "catch all" provision in the event that a duty exists in relation to vehicles, plants or equipment and is not already covered by any of the other categories.

2.05.4 *(d) Persons in Custody*
This provides that a duty of care owed to a person being held or detained in the circumstances set out in subs.(2) above is a relevant duty of care for the purposes of the Act.
The extension of the provisions of the Act to deaths in custody almost derailed the Bill, which was saved by a last minute concession by the House of Commons in June 2007. A compromise was agreed to the effect that this section of the Act will not come into force on April 6, 2008. Implementation of this part of the Act is likely to be delayed for between three to five years *(Guide to the Corporate Manslaughter and Corporate Homicide Act,* p.3). The government sought to justify deaths in custody being excluded from the scope of the Act because of "the unique set of factors contributing to the safe running of prisons" and risk factors such as substance abuse or mental health problems. Such arguments seem relevant to determining whether there has been gross negligence rather than supporting the removal of a duty of care.
The government intention is that the offence will not apply to deaths caused by suicide or acts of violence, but only workplace factors (see *Hansard*, HL, col.GC199 (January 15, 2007)).

2.06 *Subsection (3)*
To be a relevant duty of care it must come within one of the categories in s.2(1)(a)–(d) and not be excluded by any of ss.3–7.

2.07 *Subsection (4)*
This ensures that the offence will apply where a duty, previously owed under the law of negligence, has been replaced with a form of statutory strict liability, such as the liability of carriers under the Carriage of Air Act 1961.

2.08 *Subsection (5)*
Whether a relevant duty of care existed between an organisation and the deceased is a matter of law to be determined by the judge in accordance with general principles of the law of negligence.

2.09 *Subsection (6)*
For the avoidance of doubt, the Act expressly provides that common law principles preventing a duty of care being owed on the basis that the deceased voluntarily accepted the risks involved in the activity *(volenti non fit injuria)* or that the parties were jointly engaged in an illegal enterprise *(ex turpi causa non oritur actio)*, such as illegal employment, do not apply. Such concepts are not appropriate in a matter of criminal conduct.

Public policy decisions, exclusively public functions and statutory inspections

3.01 **3.**—(1) Any duty of care owed by a public authority in respect of a decision as to matters of public policy (including in particular the allocation of public resources or the weighing of competing public interests) is not a "relevant duty of care".
(2) Any duty of care owed in respect of things done in the exercise of an exclusively public function is not a "relevant duty of care" unless it falls within section 2(1)(a) , (b) or (d).
(3) Any duty of care owed by a public authority in respect of inspections carried out in the exercise of a statutory function is not a "relevant duty of care" unless it falls within section 2(1)(a) or (b).
(4) In this section—

"exclusively public function" means a function that falls within the prerogative of the Crown or is, by its nature, exercisable only with
authority conferred—
(a) by the exercise of that prerogative, or
(b) by or under a statutory provision;
"statutory function" means a function conferred by or under a statutory
provision.

DEFINITIONS

Definition of "public authority" in s.25: Section 6 of the Human Rights Act 1998 defines **3.02**
public authority as, "any person certain of whose
functions are functions of a public nature but does
not include either House of Parliament or a person
exercising functions in connection with proceedings in Parliament". Section 6(5) states that, "[i]n
relation to a particular act, a person is not a public
authority ... if the nature of the act is private".

GENERAL COMMENTARY:

Public Policy decisions are wholly exempted from the new offence. The exercise of an **3.03**
"exclusively public function" attracts only partial exemption in that duties owed as an employer
or occupier are relevant for the purposes of the Act.

Subsection (1) Matters of Public Policy **3.04**
How far the exemption extends in relation to allocation of funds and competing public
interests is not clear. The exemption applies to strategic funding decisions which require consideration of competing public interests but not to management decisions about how resources
are managed (*Guide to the Corporate Manslaughter and Corporate Homicide Act*, p.9). This
suggests that a failure to allocate funds to the NHS would not be subject to the Act but a health
trust's policy decisions may be covered.
See *Barrett v Enfield LBC* [2001] 2 A.C. 550, regarding limits of duty where allocating public
resources or weighing competing public interests.
Section 3(1) covers decisions taken by public authorities (as defined by the Human Rights Act
1998) which includes government departments, local authorities and other bodies with public
functions. The exemption is intended to reflect the position under the English common law and
is justified on the basis that there are other more appropriate "accountability mechanisms"
available (Cm. 6497, paras 18–21).

Subsection (2) Exclusively Public Functions **3.05**
This covers intrinsically public functions to the extent that they would otherwise come within
the relevant categories of s.2. Organisations are only liable for breach of a relevant duty of care
in respect of their duties as an employer or occupier of premises and not in respect of anything
done in exercise of an "exclusively public function" (defined in s.3(4) as a function exercised
under the prerogative of the Crown or a statutory provision). It is the function which determines whether the exemption applies, not the body. Accordingly, private bodies performing the
relevant type of function will also be covered. It is the nature of the activity which determines
the matter. Services relating to the function of detaining prisoners are covered even where a
private organisation carries that out on behalf of the state because the function of lawfully
detaining an individual requires statutory powers.
The government views drug licensing, issuing of driving licences and granting of planning
permission as exclusively public in nature, whereas provision of medical treatment is not, albeit
the NHS provides treatment under a statutory framework. Exemption does not extend to
activities ancillary to the public function, e.g. prison catering (*Hansard*, HL, col.GC183 (January 15, 2007)).
An activity is not exempt simply because the organisation carrying out the function is provided with statutory powers, as with NHS bodies or local authorities, but must intrinsically
require statutory or prerogative authority (e.g. licensing drugs); nor are activities exempt simply
because they require a licence (e.g. selling alcohol)(*Guide to the Corporate Manslaughter and
Corporate Homicide Act*, p.10). The activity must be of a type that cannot be independently
performed by a private body.

Private companies that exercise public functions are to be treated in the same way as public authorities exercising the same function (*Guide to the Corporate Manslaughter and Corporate Homicide Act*, p.10).

It is not clear whether the qualification "otherwise than in the exercise of an exclusively public function" applies to all the sub-clauses or just (c) and (d).

The exemption applies not simply to functions carried on under the prerogative of the Crown, but any function which "by its nature" is carried on with the relevant statutory authority. The government's intention is that it applies to services such as prison service where the prison is operated by a commercial organisation on the government's behalf (Cm. 6497, para.22).[3]

3.06 *Subsection (3) Statutory inspections*

Section 3(3) limits duties of care in respect of statutory inspections to those owed as an employer or occupier of premises. The exemption covers inspections conducted by regulatory authorities, such as the Health and Safety Executive, in exercise of statutory duties to ensure compliance with relevant standards.

The government states that the intended effect of the exemption in s.3 is "to create a broad level playing field between public and private sectors. Both are treated in the same way in their roles as employers and occupiers of premises and when providing goods and services or operating commercially. But the offence does not apply to activities that the private sector either does not do, or cannot do without particular lawful authority" (Cm. 6497 para.24).

Military activities

4.01 **4.**—(1) Any duty of care owed by the Ministry of Defence in respect of—
(a) operations within subsection (2),
(b) activities carried on in preparation for, or directly in support or, such operations, or
(c) training of a hazardous nature, or training carried out in a hazardous way, which it is considered needs to be carried out, or carried out in that way, in order to improve or maintain the effectiveness of the armed forces with respect to such operations,
is not a "relevant duty of care".

(2) The operations within this subsection are operations, including peacekeeping operations and operations for dealing with terrorism, civil unrest or serious public disorder, in the course of which members of the armed forces come under attack or face the treat of attack or violent resistance.

(3) Any duty of care owed by the Ministry of Defence in respect of activities carried on by members of the special forces is not a "relevant duty of care".

(4) In this section "the special forces" means those units of the armed forces the maintenance of whose capabilities is the responsibility of the Director of Special Forces or which are for the time being subject to the operational command of that Director.

DEFINITIONS

4.02 "the armed forces" s.25: means any of the naval, military or air forces of the Crown raised under the law of the United Kingdom (s.12).

GENERAL COMMENTARY

4.03 The exemption under s.4 is a full exemption and covers military combat activities, whether related to war, peacekeeping, terrorism or violent disorder.

---

[3] One commentator has queried whether the exemption would apply to the activities of local authorities whose functions are entirely exercised in accordance with authority conferred by or under a statutory enactment: advice of David Travers for The Centre For Corporate Accountability, May, 2005 (*www.corporateaccountability.org* [Accessed February 22, 2008]; *Hansard*, HL, cols GC224–225 (January 15, 2007)). This has been subject to criticism as an "illogical and arbitrary exemption"

Certain military activities will also be exempt under the partial exemption in s.3(2), but s.4 provides an additional exemption in relation to duties owed as an employer or occupier.

Activities conducted in preparation for, or in support of, combat activities are also covered by the exemption. This would probably not extend to activities such as basic recruit training, training for new roles or equipment, adventurous training (as opposed to "hazardous" training, which is covered) or testing and routine maintenance of equipment, but may cover organisation of deployment immediately prior to combat, reconnaissance missions, the establishment of supply chains and live fire training (*Hansard*, HL, col.GC230 (January 17, 2007) for the debate on the scope of the exemption).[4]

The Act does not apply where the harm resulting in death occurs overseas, unless it occurs in a British registered ship or aircraft. The Health and Safety Executive ("the HSE") takes the view that the HSWA may apply to Ministry of Defence decisions and their ramifications where taken inside the United Kingdom, notwithstanding that any harmful incident resulting from the decision occurs outwith the jurisdiction (*www.hse.gov.uk/services/armedforces* [Accessed February 22, 2008]).

Policing and law enforcement

5.—(1) Any duty of care owed by a public authority in respect of—   **5.01**
  (a) operations within subsection (2),
  (b) activities carried on in preparation for, or directly in support of, such operations, or
  (c) training of a hazardous nature, or training carried out in a hazardous way, which it is considered needs to be carried out, or carried out in that way, in order to improve or maintain the effectiveness of officers or employees of the public authority with respect to such operations,
is not a "relevant duty of care".
  (2) The operations are within this subsection if—
  (a) they are operations for dealing with terrorism, civil unrest or serious disorder,
  (b) they involve the carrying on of policing or law-enforcement activities, and
  (c) the officers or employees of the public authority in question come under attack or face the threat of attack or violent resistance, in the course of the operations.
  (3) Any duty of care owed by a public authority in respect of other policing or law- enforcement activities is not a "relevant duty of care" unless it falls within section 2(1)(a), (b) or (d).
  In this section—
  "policing or law-enforcement activities" includes—
      (a) activities carried on in the exercise of functions that are—
          (i) functions of police forces, or
          (ii) functions of the same or a similar nature exercisable by public authorities other than police forces;
      (b) activities carried on in the exercise of functions of constables employed by a public authority;
      (c) activities carried on in the exercise of functions exercisable under Chapter 4 of Part 2 of the Serious Organised Crime and Police Act 2005 (c.15) (protection of witnesses and other persons);
      (d) activities carried on to enforce any provision contained in or made under the Immigration Acts.

---

[4] See *Multiple Claimants v MOD* [2003] EWHC 1134 (Q.B.) (or *www.hmcourts-service.-gov.uk* [Accessed February 22, 2008]): there is no duty to devise or maintain a safe system of working for personnel engaged with the enemy, planning and preparing for such operations or peacekeeping where attack is possible.

Corporate Manslaughter and Corporate Homicide Act 2007

DEFINITIONS:

5.02 "Public Authority", s.25: refers to s.6 Human Rights Act 1998 (disregarding s.6(3)(a) and (4)): "any person certain of whose functions are functions of a public nature, but does not include either House of Parliament or a person exercising functions in connection with proceedings in Parliament". Section 6(5) states that: "[i]n relation to a particular act, a person is not a public authority ... if the nature of the act is private".

"Police force": s.13(1).

GENERAL COMMENTARY

5.03 The government's intention was that the Act should apply to the police in relation to their duties as employers and owners of property but not where they are engaged in policing activities (*Hansard*, HL (January 17, 2007)). Accordingly, the police authorities owe duties to police officers and other employees and where they occupy premises, but not otherwise to the public, in relation to policing or law enforcement operations. In relation to those operations within subs.(2) above, the police authority would owe no duties at all under the Act, not even to their own employees.[5]

5.04 *Subsection (1)*

No relevant duty of care is owed by a public authority in relation to any operations listed in subs.(2) or activities in preparation for or support of such operations or hazardous training in relation to them.

"Hazardous training" is not defined but it is intended that it be interpreted narrowly (see *Hansard*, HL, col.GC241 (January 17, 2007)) and that it only covers training which is in itself hazardous or must necessarily be carried out in a hazardous way. It is not intended to apply to training which involves avoidable hazards or where training is carried out in a hazardous way because of negligence.

Activities conducted in preparation for, or in support of, the relevant operations are also covered but not activities such as basic recruit training, training for new roles or equipment, adventurous training (as opposed to "hazardous" training, which is covered) or testing and routine maintenance of equipment. The exemption probably covers organisation of deployment immediately prior to operations, reconnaissance missions, the establishment of supply chains and live fire training (*Hansard*, HL, col.GC230 (January 17, 2007)).

5.05 *Subsection (2)*

The operations wholly excluded from the duty of care are those which deal with terrorism, civil unrest or serious disorder, involving policing or law enforcement activities and where there is an attack or threat of an attack, or violent resistance. In these circumstances, the public authority owes no duties under the Act.

An operation dealing with terrorism where there is no attack or violent resistance would not be excluded by s.5(2), unless there is a reasonable basis for believing that the officers or employees in question were facing such a threat.

5.06 *Subsection (3)*

In relation to all other policing or law enforcement activities, a relevant duty of care is owed under s.2(1)(a), (b) or (d).

5.07 *Subsection (4)*

"Policing or law enforcement activities" is defined in subs.(4) as including activities carried on as functions of the police forces or similar functions exercised by other public authorities, activities of constables employed by a public authority, activities under Ch.4 of Pt 2 of the Serious Organised Crime and Police Act 2005[6] in relation to the protection of witnesses and other persons and activities carried on to enforce immigration laws.[7]

---

[5] Police forces also owe duties under the Health and Safety at Work Act 1974.

[6] Under Ch.4 of Pt 2 of the Serious Organised Crime and Police Act 2005, various authorities are empowered to make arrangements for the protection of persons involved in investigations or proceedings where the person's safety is at risk (s.82).

[7] There is an agreement between the HSE, the Home Office and Association of Chief Police Officers (2000) regarding controls in relation to hazardous training.

Emergencies

6.—(1) Any duty of care owed by an organisation within subsection (2) in **6.01** respect of the way in which it responds to emergency circumstances is not a "relevant duty of care" unless it falls within section 2(1)(a) or (b).

(2) The organisations within this subsection are—

(a) a fire and rescue authority in England and Wales;

(b) a fire and rescue authority or joint fire and rescue board in Scotland;

(c) the Northern Ireland Fire and Rescue Service Board;

(d) any other organisation providing a service of responding to emergency circumstances either—

    (i) in pursuance of arrangements made with an organisation within paragraph (a), (b) or (c), or

    (ii) (if not in pursuance of such arrangements) otherwise than on a commercial basis;

(e) a relevant NHS body;

(f) an organisation providing ambulance services in pursuance of arrangements—

    (i) made by, or at the request of, a relevant NHS body; or

    (ii) made with the Secretary of State or with the Welsh Ministers;

    (iii) an organisation providing services for the transport of organs, blood, equipment or personnel in pursuance of arrangements of the kind mentioned in paragraph (f)

    (iv) an organisation providing a rescue service;

    (v) the armed forces.

(3) For the purposes of subsection 1, the way in which an organisation responds to emergency circumstances does not include the way in which—

(a) medical treatment is carried out, or

(b) decisions within subsection (4) are made.

(4) The decisions within this subsection are decisions as to the carrying out of medical treatment, other than decisions as to the order in which persons are to be given such treatment.

(5) Any duty of care owed in respect of the carrying out, or attempted carrying out, of a rescue operation at sea in emergency circumstances is not a "relevant duty of care" unless it falls within section 2(1)(a) or (b).

(6) Any duty of care owed in respect of action taken—

(a) in order to comply with a direction under Schedule 3A to the Merchant Shipping Act 1995 (c.21) (safety directions), or

(b) by virtue of paragraph 4 of that Schedule (action in lieu of direction), is not a "relevant duty of care" unless it falls within section 2(1)(a) or (b).

(7) In this section—

"emergency circumstances" means circumstances that are present or imminent and—

(a) are causing, or are likely to cause, serious harm or a worsening of such harm, or

(b) are likely to cause the death of a person;

"medical treatment" includes any treatment or procedure of a medical or similar nature;

"relevant NHS body" means—

(a) a Strategic Health Authority, Primary Care Trust, NHS Trust, Special Health Authority, NHS Foundation Trust in England;

(b) a or Local Health Board, NHS Trust or Special Health Authority in Wales;

(c) a Health Board or Special Health Board in Scotland, or the Common Services Agency for the Scottish Health Service;

(d) a Health and Social Services trust or Health and Social Services Board in Northern Ireland;

"serious harm" means—
  (a) serious injury to or the serious illness (including mental illness) of a person;
  (b) serious harm to the environment (including the life and health of plants and animals);
  (c) serious harm to any building or other property.
(8) A reference in this section to emergency circumstances includes a reference to circumstances that are believed to be emergency circumstances.

6.02 DEFINITIONS
"Emergency circumstances": subss.(7) and (8).

GENERAL COMMENTARY
6.03 *Subsection (1)*
The organisations listed in subs.(2) only owe relevant duties of care to their employees or those working for, or performing services for the organisation, or in its capacity as an occupier of premises when responding to "emergency circumstances".

No relevant duty of care is owed by the relevant organisations to those in receipt of the emergency service or to third parties affected by the emergency response. Note also that the nature of the emergency response is not limited to matters of personal injury but includes action taken to prevent environmental damage, harm to animals and damage to property.

The relevant organisations owe no duties of care under s.2(1)(c) and (d) notwithstanding that, under the common law, they may, in limited circumstances, owe such duties. Whilst for public policy reasons, the emergency and rescue services are generally not regarded as owing a duty of care in relation to their actions and omissions during an emergency response, that is based on the proposition that they are not generally responsible for causing the danger or emergency to which they are responding.[8]

6.04 *Subsection (2)*
The organisations entitled to the exemption in subs.(1) are as follows:

6.04.1 *Fire and Rescue Services*
In Scotland that is the relevant local council in accordance with s.1 of the Fire (Scotland) Act 2005. In relation to England and Wales, it is the relevant local authority under s.1 of the Fire and Rescue Services Act 2004 and in Northern Ireland the board established under the Fire and Rescue Services (Northern Ireland) Order 2006.

Subsection (2)(d) extends the exemption to organisations providing an emergency response on behalf of the relevant fire and rescue authorities or boards or to any other organisation providing an emergency response service provided it is done on a non-commercial basis. In light of the wide definition of "emergency circumstances" this would appear to extend beyond those types of emergency response services typically offered by fire and rescue services, provided the service is not being offered on a commercial basis.

6.04.2 *National Health Service*
The relevant NHS body is defined in subs.(7).

---

[8] See, however, *Derek Burnett v Grampian Fire and Rescue Service*, 2007 S.L.T. 61 where Lord Macphail held that Grampian Fire and Rescue Service owed a duty of care to take all reasonable steps not only to extinguish the fire (which occurred in the flat below that of Mr Burnett) but also to prevent the fire re-igniting and causing damage to his neighbouring property. Where the emergency or rescue service negligently creates a new or different danger whilst responding to an emergency a duty of care would also generally exist at common law: see *Capital and Counties v Hampshire cc Court of Appeal* [1997] QB1004, [1997] W.L.R. 331, [1997] All E.R. 865 in relation to the fire service duty of care; *Costello v Chief Constable of Northumbria Police* [1999] 1 All E.R. 5550 in relation to the police; *OLL Limited v S of S for Transport* [1997] 3 All E.R. 897 in relation to the coast guard; and *Kent v Griffiths* [2000] 2 All E.R. 474 in relation to the ambulance service.

Ambulance Service **6.04.3**

An organisation providing ambulance services on behalf of, or at the request of, a relevant NHS body is entitled to rely on the duty of care limitation. Accordingly, those providing private ambulance services under contract to the NHS will be covered in relation to such services but not otherwise. When providing ambulance services in the private sector, the organisations owe a duty of care in accordance with the additional sub-categories of s.2(1).

Transportation of Organs, Blood, Equipment or Personnel **6.04.4**

An organisation providing these services on behalf of, or at the request of a relevant NHS body is entitled to rely on the duty of care limitation. Accordingly, those transporting under contract to the NHS will be covered in relation to such services but not otherwise. When transporting in the private sector, the organisations will owe a duty of care in accordance with the additional sub-categories of s.2(1).

Rescue Services **6.04.5**

An organisation providing a rescue service is entitled to the benefit of the duty of care limitation. "Rescue service" is not defined in the Act. The exemption does not appear to be limited to organisations providing the service on a non-commercial basis. Accordingly, organisations which would not qualify for the exemption under subs.(d)(ii) may well qualify under subs.(b). The term "rescue" possibly limits the scope of this exemption to those providing assistance to individuals and not to attempts to save the environment or property.

Subsections (3) and (4) Medical Treatment **6.05**

In relation to the provision of medical treatment, the partial exemption extends only to decisions about the order in which persons are to receive treatment. Accordingly, a relevant duty of care is owed in relation to the carrying out of medical treatment and any other decisions relating to such treatment.

Subsection (5) Rescues at Sea **6.06**

An organisation carrying out a rescue operation at sea in emergency circumstances is entitled to the benefit of the exemption. The explicit reference to the defined term "emergency circumstances" suggests that this exemption also extends to emergencies relating to environmental or property damage and so may include the rescue of property or wildlife. Accordingly a salvage operation might be capable of coming within the terms of the exemption. Unlike subs.(d)(ii), the exemption under subs.(5) appears to apply whether or not the rescue operation is being conducted on a commercial basis. Offshore operators who are required to make arrangements for rescue at sea, in terms of the Offshore Installations (Prevention of Fire and Explosion, and Emergency Response) Regulations 1995, may also be covered by the exemption in relation to third parties affected by their operations. Those on the installation or otherwise performing services for the operator would be owed a relevant duty of care under s.2(1)(a).

Subsection (6) **6.07**

Schedule 3A to the Merchant Shipping Act 1995 empowers the Secretary of State to give a direction to various parties, including the owner or master of a ship, or those engaged in a salvage operation, in relation to the ship or those on board where an accident has occurred which has created a risk to safety or of pollution. Failure to comply with such a direction is a criminal offence (Sch.3A, para.6(1)).

Child protection and probation

7.—(1) A duty of care to which this section applies is not a "relevant duty **7.01** of care" unless it falls within section 2(1)(a) (b) or (d).

(2) This section applies to any duty of care that a local authority or other public authority owes in respect of the exercise by it of functions conferred by or under—

(a) Parts 4 and 5 of the Children Act 1989 (c.41),

(b) Part 2 of the Children (Scotland) Act 1995 (c.36), or

(c) Parts 5 and 6 of the Children (Northern Ireland) Order 1995 (S.I. 1995/755 (N.I.2)),

(3) This section also applies to any duty of care that a local probation board or other public authority owes in respect of the exercise by it of functions conferred by or under—

(a) Chapter 1 of Part 1 of the Criminal Justice and Court Services Act 2000 (c.43),
(b) section 27, of the Social Work (Scotland) Act 1968 (c.49), or
(c) Article 4 of the Probation Board (Northern Ireland) Order 1982 (S.I. 1982/713 (N.I.10)).

DEFINITIONS

7.02 "Employee" is defined in s.25: means an individual who works under a contract of employment or apprenticeship (whether express or implied and, if express, whether oral or in writing) and related expressions are to be construed accordingly.

"Public authority" is defined in s.25: which refers to s.6 of the Human Rights Act 1998. This defines public authority as, "any person certain of whose functions are functions of a public nature but does not include either House of Parliament or a person exercising functions in connection with proceedings in Parliament". Section 6(5) states that, "[i]n relation to a particular act, a person is not a public authority ... if the nature of the act is private".

GENERAL COMMENTARY

7.03 *Subsection (1)*

Local or public authorities exercising functions conferred under the statutes listed in subs.(2) only owe duties of care to their employees, those working for the authority or those performing services for it, or in its capacity as an occupier of premises.

Accordingly no relevant duty of care is owed by the local or public authority to those otherwise affected by the exercise of the relevant child protection functions. In particular, there is no relevant duty of care in relation to the children under the care or supervision of the relevant authority, other than in its capacity as an occupier of premises.

7.04 *Subsection (2)*

In Scotland, local authorities owe duties to any child looked after by them in order to safeguard and promote the child's welfare (s.17 The Children (Scotland) Act 1995). The Act also contains powers in relation to compulsory supervision and child protection orders.

7.05 *Subsection (3)*

Probation boards or other public authorities are similarly exempt from duties other than in the capacity as employer or occupier in relation to its functions under s.27 of the Social Work (Scotland) Act 1968. That section provides that local authorities must provide a service for the following purposes:

(a) The provision of social background reports for courts and other reports for children's hearings, the procurator fiscal or the Lord Advocate.
(b) The supervision of, and advice, guidance and assistance for, those placed under a supervision order by the courts or following release from prison or other form of detention. Supervision also extends to persons subject to a community service order under s.238 of the Criminal Procedure (Scotland) Act 1995 or a probation order which includes a requirement to perform unpaid work and to supervised attendance orders under s.235 of the 1995 Act; persons subject to the supervision and treatment order under s.57(2)(d) of the Criminal Procedure (Scotland) Act 1995. Each local authority is required to prepare a probation, community service and supervised attendance scheme confirming the relevant arrangements to be made.

Gross Breach

Factors for jury

8.—(1) This section applies where—   **8.01**
  (a) it is established that an organisation owed a relevant duty of care to a
     person, and
  (b) it falls to the jury to decide whether there was a gross breach of that
     duty.
(2) The jury must consider whether the evidence shows that the organisation failed to comply with any health and safety legislation that relates to
the alleged breach, and if so—
  (a) how serious that failure was;
  (b) how much of a risk of death it posed.
(3) The jury may also—
  (a) consider the extent to which the evidence shows that there were
     attitudes, policies, systems or accepted practices within the organi-
     sation that were likely to have encouraged any such failure as is
     mentioned in subsection (2), or to have produced tolerance of it;
  (b) have regard to any health and safety guidance that relates to the
     alleged breach.
(4) This section does not prevent the jury from having regard to any other
matters they consider relevant.
(5) In this section "health and safety guidance" means any code, guidance,
manual or similar publication that is concerned with health and safety
matters and is made or issued (under a statutory provision or otherwise) by
an authority responsible for the enforcement of any health and safety
legislation.

DEFINITIONS
  "organisation": s.1(2)   **8.02**
  "relevant duty of care": s.2, read with ss.3–7
  "gross breach": s.1(4)(b)
  "health and safety legislation": s.25
  "statutory provision": s.25

GENERAL COMMENTARY
  "Gross breach" is defined in s.1(4)(b) and the meaning of the term is considered in the **8.03**
commentary on that part of the Act (see paras 1.08 and 1.09). Section 8 provides guidance for
the jury in determining whether any breach of a relevant duty of care amounts to a "gross"
breach.
  Section 8(1) makes it clear that a jury will only require to consider whether an organisation
has been guilty of a gross breach of duty if the Crown has already established that the organisation owed a relevant duty of care. Whether a particular organisation owes a duty of care is a
question of law and the trial judge must make any findings of fact necessary to decide that
question (s.2(5)—for commentary, see para.2.08).
  Section 8(1)(b) establishes that it will be for the jury to determine whether there has been a
breach of a relevant duty of care and, if so, whether that breach was a "gross" breach. A breach
will be "gross" if the conduct alleged to amount to a breach of that duty falls *far* (our emphasis)
below what can reasonably be expected of the organisation in the circumstances.
  In determining whether there has been a gross breach of duty, s.8(2) sets out the matters to **8.04**
which the jury *must* (our emphasis) have regard and subs.(3) and (4) set out matters to which the
jury is *entitled*(our emphasis) to have regard. In respect of all these matters, the jury is required
to measure any conclusions which it reaches which are adverse to the organisation against the
standard below which the conduct of the organisation would require to have fallen to amount
to a "gross" breach of duty, namely "far below" (see commentary on s.1(4)(b), para.1.09).
  Section 8(2) states that the jury *must* (our emphasis) consider whether the evidence reveals a
failure on the part of the organisation to have complied with any health and safety legislation
relating to the alleged breach and, if so, how serious the failure was and how much of a risk of

death it posed. "Health and safety legislation" is defined in s.25 as meaning "any statutory provision dealing with health and safety matters, including in particular provision contained in the Health and Safety at Work Act 1974".

8.05   If in any particular case the jury has concluded that the organisation has failed to comply with health and safety legislation relating to the alleged breach, subs.(3)(a) entitles the jury to go on to consider a number of issues which can, perhaps, best be summarised as the "culture" of an organisation, and to consider whether there were "attitudes, policies, systems or accepted practices within the organisation" which would have been likely to have either encouraged or produced tolerance of the failure by the organisation. "Attitudes", "accepted practices" and "likely to have either encouraged or produced tolerance" are vague terms, no guidance is provided in the Act by way of interpretation and in these circumstances will be issues which will be particularly difficult for a jury to determine.

8.06   Subsection (3)(b) entitles the jury to have regard to any health and safety guidance that relates to the alleged breach in assessing the extent, if any, of the breach. "Health and safety guidance" is defined in subs.(5) and is sufficiently broad in its terms to encompass almost any publication concerned with health and safety matters which has been made or issued by the HSE, HSC or other authority responsible for the enforcement of any health and safety legislation. This position is to be contrasted with criminal proceedings under the HSWA in which, although evidence of such publications may be admissible, the evidential significance of health and safety guidance is restricted to approved codes of practice (see HSWA, ss.16–17).

One example of "guidance", to which a jury is very likely to be urged to have regard by the prosecution in relation to the conduct of senior management, is the joint guidance published in October 2007 by the Institute of Directors ("the IOD") and the Health and Safety Commission ("the HSC"), *Leading health and safety at work: Leadership Actions for Directors and Board Members* (see Appendix 3). Its contents reveal that both the IOD and HSC clearly had the CMCHA in mind when considering its terms (see *www.hse.gov.uk/leadership* [Access February 22, 2008]). Although it is not obligatory for directors to comply with the guidance, any failure to follow it is likely to be founded upon by the prosecution in proceedings brought under the Act.

In its introduction the authors state:

> "Protecting the health and safety of employees or members of the public who may be affected by your activities is an essential part of risk management and must be led by the board. Failure to include health and safety as a key business risk in board decisions can have catastrophic results. Many high-profile safety cases over the years have been rooted in failures of leadership. Health and safety law places duties on organisations and employers, and directors can be personally liable when these duties are breached: members of the board have both collective and individual responsibility for health and safety. By following this guidance, you will help your organisation find the best ways to lead and promote health and safety, and therefore meet its legal obligations."

Interestingly, in its research report on the health and safety responsibilities of company directors and management board members published in 2006, the HSE found, following surveys conducted over the period of 2001 to2005, that:

> "[W]hilst only a minority of directors and managers spontaneously cite defining duties in law as an effective method, the majority think defining duties in law would be useful, and only a small minority believe this would have negative consequences in respect of deterring people from being directors or making health and safety matter of liability management."
> (*www.hse.gov.uk/research/rrhtm/rr414.htm* [Accessed February 22, 2008].)

8.07   It will be interesting to see how broadly subs.(5) is interpreted. For example, in July 2005 the HSE launched its Corporate Health and Safety Performance Index ("CHaSPI"). The purpose of CHaSPI, a web based assessment tool, is described as being to "allow organisations to measure, benchmark and report their health and safety performance...and helps draw senior management attention to health and safety performance"(Health and Safety Executive, *Corporate Health and Safety Performance Index: OSH Professionals Information Sheet, www.chaspi. info-exchange.com* [accessed March 11, 2008]). Clearly, there is no obligation on an organisation to use CHaSPI. However, it remains to be seen whether CHaSPI itself, or the failure to use such tools in monitoring health and safety performance is something to which a jury would be entitled to have regard, whether as "a similar publication" under subs.(5) or "any other matter they consider relevant" under subs.(4).

Subsection (4) permits the jury to have regard to any other matters they consider relevant when assessing the extent of the breach of the relevant duty of care. The wording of the subsection is unqualified but, it is submitted, must be restricted to matters which have been adduced in evidence and, arguably, in respect of which notice has been given in the indictment. In the draft Corporate Manslaughter Bill (Cm. 6497) presented to Parliament in March 2005, included in the issues to be considered by a jury when determining whether a breach was "gross" was "whether or not senior managers of the organisation knew, or ought to have known that the organisation was failing to comply with that legislation or guidance; were aware, or ought to have been aware, of the risk of death or serious harm posed by the failure to comply; sought to cause the organisation to profit from that failure". Although these issues do not feature in the Act, they are examples of the types of issue which a jury may well consider to be relevant when assessing the standard of conduct of an organisation.[9]

Remedial orders

Power to order breach etc to be remedied

9.—(1) A court before which an organisation is convicted of corporate **9.01** manslaughter or corporate homicide may make an order (a "remedial order") requiring the organisation to take specified steps to remedy—
  (a) the breach mentioned in section 1(1) ("the relevant breach");
  (b) any matter that appears to the court to have resulted from the relevant breach and to have been a cause of the death;
  (c) any deficiency, as regards health and safety matters, in the organisation's policies, systems or practices of which the relevant breach appears to the court to be an indication.
  (2) A remedial order may be made only on an application by the prosecution specifying the terms of the proposed order.
Any such order must be on such terms (whether those proposed or others) as the court considers appropriate having regard to any representations made, and any evidence adduced, in relation to that matter by the prosecution or on behalf of the organisation.
  (3) Before making an application for a remedial order the prosecution must consult such enforcement authority or authorities as it considers appropriate having regard to the nature of the relevant breach.
  (4) A remedial order—
  (a) must specify a period within which the steps referred to in subsection (1) are to be taken.
  (b) May require the organisation to supply to an enforcement authority consulted under subsection (3), within a specified period, evidence that those steps have been taken.
A period specified under this subsection may be extended or further extended by order of the court on an application made before the end of that period or extended period.
  (5) An organisation that fails to comply with a remedial order is guilty of an offence, and liable on conviction on indictment to a fine.

DEFINITIONS
  "organisation": s.1(2)   **9.02**
  "remedial order": s.25
  "enforcement authority": s.25

---

[9] It is very likely that account will be taken of industry guidance in many cases. (See commentary on s.1 at para.1.09 for analysis of evidential significance of industry guidance).

GENERAL NOTE

9.03 The power given to the court by virtue of s.9 is similar to the power given to the court under s.42 of the HSWA following conviction of an offence under that Act. However, there are certain significant differences. Unlike the power under s.42, the court only has power to make a remedial order under s.9 if the Crown makes an application for such an order (s.9(2)). The ambit of a remedial order under s.42 is restricted to matters which formed the subject matter of the conviction, whereas a remedial order under s.9 is potentially extremely wide-ranging and onerous for the organisation. It may relate to "any deficiency as regards health and safety matters...of which the relevant breach appears to the court to be an indication" (s.9(1)(c)).

9.04 Although it is not expressly stated, unlike s.42(1) of the HSWA, it would appear that a remedial order may be imposed in addition to any fine imposed under s.1(6) and any publicity order imposed under s.10.

It is likely that remedial orders will be imposed infrequently as the regulating authorities will normally have required any deficiency to be remedied prior to the commencement of a trial by the imposition of an improvement (s.21) or prohibition notice (s.22) under the HSWA. In those cases where they are imposed, it is unlikely that any financial penalty would be reduced as a result. The SAP, asked by the Sentencing Guidelines Council in England to produce advice on sentencing in relation to an offence under the new Act, expressed its provisional view in November 2007 as follows:

> "...[T]he Panel's provisional view is that the costs involved in complying with the remedial order should not lead to a corresponding decrease in any fine imposed for the same offence. The order is rehabilitative rather than punitive, and merely requires the offender to take steps to comply with the health and safety standards already required by law. Any reduction in the fine would reward unfairly the few organisations that have resisted compliance with those standards, and would lead to inequitable treatment of the majority of organisations..." (Sentencing Advisory Panel, *Consultation Paper on Sentencing for Corporate Manslaughter*, November 15, 2007; see Appendix 4.)

It is likely that a similar conclusion will be reached by the High Court.

9.05 Subsection (5) states that an organisation that fails to comply with a remedial order is guilty of an offence and liable on conviction on indictment to a fine. Under s.33(2A) of the HSWA failure to comply with an improvement notice (s.21), prohibition notice (s.22) or a remedial order (s.42) are offences punishable, "(a) on summary conviction, to imprisonment for a term not exceeding six months, or a fine not exceeding £20,000, or both; and (b) on conviction on indictment, to imprisonment for a term not exceeding two years, or a fine, or both". The level of fine and imprisonment which can be imposed under the HSWA provides a clear indication of the serious view taken of such breaches. It follows that any offence committed under subs.(5) of the CMCHA is likely to attract very significant financial penalties.

Power to order conviction etc to be publicised

10.01   **10.**—(1) A court before which an organisation is convicted of corporate manslaughter or corporate homicide may make an order (a "publicity order") requiring the organisation to publicise in a specified manner—

(a) the fact that it has been convicted of the offence;
(b) specified particulars of the offence;
(c) the amount of any fine imposed;
(d) the terms of any remedial order made.

(2) In deciding on the terms of a publicity order that it is proposing to make, the court must—

(a) ascertain the views of such enforcement authority or authorities (if any) as it considers appropriate, and
(b) have regard to any representations made by the prosecution or on behalf of the organisation.

(3) A publicity order—

(a) must specify a period within which the requirements referred to in subsection (1) are to be complied with;
(b) supply to any enforcement authority whose views have been ascer-

tained under subsection (2), within a specified period, evidence that those requirements have been complied with.

(4) An organisation that fails to comply with a publicity order is guilty of an offence, and liable on conviction on indictment to a fine.

DEFINITIONS
  "organisation" : s.1(2)
  "enforcement authority": s.25

10.02

GENERAL NOTE

The power to impose a publicity order upon an organisation arises only where there has been **10.03** a conviction for corporate homicide (s.10(1)). The power does not exist if an organisation is convicted of a lesser offence under the HSWA.

Unlike the imposition of a remedial order, the court is entitled to make such an order if it considers it appropriate and is not dependent upon an application being made by the prosecution for such an order. Indeed, the prosecution is given no power to make an application for a publicity order. Further, it is only where the court has already reached a decision to impose a publicity order that the court is then required, when deciding on the terms of a proposed order, to ascertain the views of such enforcement authorities as it considers appropriate (s.10(2)(a)), and to have regard to any representations made by the prosecution or on behalf of the organisation (s.10(2)(b).

Publicity Orders are a new sanction in health and safety law in the United Kingdom and only **10.04** found their way onto the statute book at a very late stage, having been introduced by way of amendment when the Bill was at Report stage in the House of Lords in February 2007. Official publicity by the safety regulator of convictions under the HSWA has been restricted in the past to the maintenance by the HSE of a public database on its website containing details of all organisations convicted under the HSWA since 2000. Since October 2001 the database has been extended to include all organisations which have been the subject of improvement and prohibition notices served under the HSWA. At present, it is not clear how often and in what particular circumstances publicity orders will be imposed. It may be thought that, having regard to the likely degree of media attention which would be given to any conviction for an offence of corporate homicide, that a publicity order would be rendered somewhat superfluous.[10]

However, the issue of sentencing generally in relation to the new Act is a matter upon which **10.05** the SAP in England has been asked by the Sentencing Guidelines Council to advise. The panel published a consultation paper in November 2007 in which it stated that:

> "[T]he Panel is consulting on sentencing for both corporate manslaughter and breaches of health and safety law that result in death, in order to promote consistency and to produce guidelines that properly reflect the seriousness of the offending involved." (SAP, *Consultation Paper*, November 15, 2007, Appendix 4.)

In relation to publicity orders, the panel has concluded that a publicity order should be made in **10.06** every case where there is a conviction for corporate manslaughter/homicide. It set out its views in the following terms:

> "The order is primarily intended as an additional deterrent designed to put offenders at a disadvantage in comparison with competitors who do not break the law. The Law Reform Commission of New South Wales has suggested that publicity orders may lose their efficacy if they are imposed on every organisation convicted of any type of offence but identified the following situations in which they might be most useful:
> - The court has reduced a fine due to the organisation's financial circumstances
> - The organisation has a poor record of compliance with the law (a publicity order may increase the pressure on the organisation to comply)

---

[10] The CCA has given qualified support to the concept of publicity orders. Its executive director, David Bergman, has stated, "[t]he CCA also believes that the current provisions in the Corporate Manslaughter and Corporate Homicide Act 2007—principally fines and publicity orders—fail to address the need for a full range of effective corporate penalties available to the courts. The new 'publicity orders' should be seen simply as a first step towards more effective sentencing reforms." (CCA press release, *Proposed Fines for Corporate Manslaughter conviction inadequate says safety charity*, November 21, 2007.)

- It is considered that the organisation's customers, creditors and/or shareholders should know about the conviction, or where news coverage is likely to be insufficient (although it might be argued that most cases of corporate manslaughter would attract publicity).

The potentially 'desensitizing' effect on the public of a regular use of publicity orders may be of less relevance to cases of corporate manslaughter. If it does serve a deterrent purpose, an order might be considered appropriate in most cases where the offender is operating in a competitive market. The Panel's provisional view is that, in principle, a publicity order should be imposed on every offender convicted of corporate manslaughter. However, there may be cases where the making of an order may be less appropriate, for example where the offender is providing a local public service in relation to which the public cannot exercise choice." (SAP, *Consultation Paper*, paras 79–80.)

10.07 *"Specified manner"*

No guidance is given in the Act regarding the "specified manner" any publicity order should take in terms of s.10(1). The SAP considered the issue in its consultation paper and expressed the following views:

"A court may order that the details of an offence are published in any 'specified manner', giving the court scope to ensure that the publicity reaches its intended audience. Options for the form of the order include:
- publication on television/radio and/or in a local/national/trade newspaper, including relevant broadcaster/newspaper websites;
- publication on the organisation's website and in its annual report, informing (potential) customers and those who might be interested in investing in the organisation;
- notice to shareholders; and
- letters to customers and/or suppliers of the organisation.

In light of the range of offenders, the Panel does not consider it sensible to seek to provide detailed guidance on the extent of publicity, but it may be possible to set some minimum standards. For example, if the offender is a local organisation, it might normally be appropriate to require publication in the local media; in the case of a large national organisation, publication in national media would be more effective. In both cases, a notice in all relevant trade journals should be required. Any shareholders should be notified in order that they may press for enhanced health and safety standards and publication should always be required in an annual report." (SAP, *Consultation Paper*, paras 81–82.)

10.08 *Relationship between making of publicity order and level of fine imposed under s.1(6)*

In its consultation paper, the SAP took the opportunity to consider the relationship between the making of a publicity order and the level of fine which may be imposed in any particular case, and whether it would be appropriate for a court, when considering the level of a fine, to have regard to whether it had in mind to impose a publicity order as well. The panel expressed its views as follows:

"The requirements of a publicity order will entail both direct and indirect costs for the offending organisation. The direct costs to the offender of placing the advertisement and notifying shareholders are likely to be relatively small and easy to calculate. The indirect costs in the form of loss of custom and/or investment are potentially much larger and more difficult to estimate. However, as the Panel's proposed starting point and range for the financial penalty are based on the premise that a publicity order will be imposed in every case of corporate manslaughter, the court should not need to give any further consideration to the effect of such an order on the overall sentence. As mentioned earlier in paragraph 59, where a publicity order is not imposed, the court should consider whether a higher fine would be appropriate."(Para.83.)

10.09 *Commencement date for Publicity Orders*

The provisions relating to publicity orders will not be introduced until the sentencing guidelines have been finalised by the Council and it is understood that this exercise is unlikely to have been completed before the autumn of 2008. Although the guidelines will obviously not apply in Scotland they are likely to be of considerable assistance to practitioners in relation to the imposition of publicity orders, and sentencing issues generally in corporate homicide and health and safety prosecutions.[11]

Application to particular categories of organisation

Application to Crown bodies

11.—(1) An organisation that is a servant or agent of the Crown is not **11.01** immune from prosecution under this Act for that reason.

(2) For the purposes of this Act—

  (a) a department or other body listed in Schedule 1, or

  (b) a corporation that is a servant or agent of the Crown,

is to be treated as owing whatever duties of care it would owe if it were a corporation that was not a servant or agent of the Crown.

(3) For the purposes of section 2—

  (a) a person who is—

     (i) employed by or under the Crown for the purposes of a department or other body listed in Schedule 1, or

     (ii) employed by a person whose staff constitute a body listed in that Schedule,

    is to be treated as employed by that department or body;

  (b) any premises occupied for the purposes of—

     (i) a department or other body listed in Schedule 1, or

     (ii) a person whose staff constitute a body listed in that Schedule,

    are to be treated as occupied by that department or body.

(4) For the purposes of sections 2 to 7 anything done purportedly by a department or other body listed in Schedule 1, although in law by the Crown or by the holder of a particular office, is to be treated as done by the department or other body itself.

(5) Subsections (3)(a)(i), (3)(b)(i) and (4) apply in relation to a Northern Ireland department as they apply in relation to a department or other body listed in Schedule 1.

GENERAL COMMENTARY

Subsection (1)   **11.02**

The general proposition that emanations of the Crown are immune from criminal prosecution does not apply. This represents a departure from the general approach to health and safety law. Whilst the Crown can be investigated by the HSE in relation to accidents at work, it cannot be prosecuted under the HSWA. Proceedings may not be taken against the Crown under the 1974 Act, but administrative procedures known as Crown Censures have been developed for use

---

[11] Sentencing guidelines do not exist in Scotland. The Sentencing Commission for Scotland, which was established by the Scottish Executive in 2005, produced its report on the scope to improve consistency in sentencing in Scotland in September 2006. In launching the report, the Commission's Chairman, the Rt Hon. Lord Macfadyen said, "[w]e have recommended the creation of a statutory body—the Advisory Panel on Sentencing in Scotland—which would be responsible for the preparation of draft sentencing guidelines for consideration by the Appeal Court of the High Court of Justiciary. The adoption of such draft guidelines, with or without modification, would be a matter for the Appeal Court. We have recommended that the APSS should contain other than the judiciary among its membership but we consider that it is important that final decisions should be for the Appeal Court in order to ensure that sentencing remains essentially a judicial function. We envisage that the introduction of sentencing guidelines would be a gradual process. Under our proposals, particular guidelines, once promulgated by the Appeal Court, would guide sentencers, but would not dictate sentences in individual cases. We have, however, recommended that where a sentencer imposes a sentence which is outwith the guidelines he or she should be required to provide an explanation for this." To date, the recommendations of the Commission have not been implemented (see commentary at para.1.12 for references to reported sentencing guideline cases in England).

in circumstances where it is the Health and Safety Executive's opinion that, but for Crown immunity, there would have been sufficient evidence to provide a realistic prospect of conviction in the courts.[12]

It has been argued that Crown immunity from liability for common law crimes, such as manslaughter and for health and safety offences causing death, gives rise to a clear risk of a breach of the European Convention on Human Rights (see Joint Opinion of Counsel, Matrix Chambers, the Centre for Corporate Accountability, December 1, 2003, *www.corporate accountability.org* [Accessed February 25, 2008]).

Under s.8 of the Act, the jury is required to consider, as a prerequisite to a finding of gross breach, whether the organisation has failed to comply with any health and safety legislation that relates to the alleged breach. Although emanations of the Crown are immune from prosecution under the 1974 Act, they are still required to comply with the provisions of the Act as the immunity relates purely to the enforcement provisions (s.48, 1974 Act).

It does raise an issue over how the jury will come to the conclusion that a breach of the HSWA, or other relevant legislation, has occurred, since there can be no separate conviction for such a breach. The Lord Advocate will not be able to bring a prosecution on the same indictment for a breach of the 1974 Act but will, nonetheless, require to prove to the satisfaction of the jury that such a breach has occurred.

11.03 *Subsection (2)*

The Act does not define what is meant by "servant or agent of the Crown". Although there is a list in Sch.1 of government departments and bodies, this does not appear to be exclusive. Subsection 2(b) recognises that a corporation may also be a servant or agent of the Crown.

Each department or body is to be treated as a separate legal entity, "owing whatever duties of care it would owe if it were a corporation". The department or body may also be an occupier and owe relevant duties as such under s.2(1)(b).

While there are no government departments or bodies excluded from the operation of s.11, there are particular exemptions in relation to certain activities in ss.3–7 of the Act (see paras 3.01–7.05).

Application to armed forces

12.01   **12.**—(1) In this Act "the armed forces" means any of the naval, military or air forces of the Crown raised under the law of the United Kingdom.

(2) For the purposes of section 2 a person who is a member of the armed forces is to be treated as employed by the Ministry of Defence.

(3) A reference in this Act to members of the armed forces includes a reference to—

  (a) members of the reserve forces (within the meaning given by section 1(2) of the Reserve Forces Act 1996 (c.14)) when in service or undertaking training or duties;

  (b) persons serving on Her Majesty's vessels (within the meaning given by section 132(1) of the Naval Discipline Act 1957 (c.53)).

DEFINITIONS

12.02   Section 1(2) Reserve Forces Act 1996: "reserve forces" means the Royal Fleet Reserve, the Royal Naval Reserve, the Royal Marines Reserve, the Army Reserve, the Territorial Army, the Air Force Reserve and the Royal Auxiliary Air Force.

GENERAL COMMENTARY

12.03   See the general commentary to s.4 in relation to the exemption of certain military operations from the scope of the offence.

Application to police forces

13.01   **13.**—(1) In this Act "police force" means—

---

[12] See Health and Safety Executive Sector Information Minute SIM07/2001/34, *www.hse.gov.uk* [Accessed February 25, 2008].

   (a) a police force within the meaning of—
       (i) the Police Act 1996 (c.16), or
      (ii) the Police (Scotland) Act 1967 (c.77);
   (b) the Police Service of Northern Ireland;
   (c) the Police Service of Northern Ireland Reserve;
   (d) the British Transport Police Force;
   (e) the Civil Nuclear Constabulary;
   (f) the Ministry of Defence Police.

(2) For the purposes of this Act a police force is to be treated as owing whatever duties of care it would owe if it were a body corporate.

(3) For the purposes of section 2—

   (a) a member of a police force is to be treated as employed by that force;
   (b) a special constable appointed for a police area in England and Wales is to be treated as employed by the police force maintained by the police authority for that area;
   (c) a special constable appointed for a police force mentioned in paragraph (d) or (f) of subsection (1) is to be treated as employed by that force;
   (d) a police cadet undergoing training with a view to becoming a member of a police force mentioned in paragraph (a) or (d) of subsection (1) is to be treated as employed by that force;
   (e) a police trainee appointed under section 39 of the Police (Northern Ireland) Act 2000 (c.32) or a police cadet appointed under section 42 of that Act is to be treated as employed by the Police Service of Northern Ireland;
   (f) a police reserve trainee appointed under section 40 of that Act is to be treated as employed by the Police Service of Northern Ireland Reserve;
   (g) a member of a police force seconded to the Serious Organised Crime Agency or the National Policing Improvement Agency to serve as a member of its staff is to be treated as employed by that Agency.

(4) A reference in subsection (3) to a member of a police force is to be read, in the case of a force mentioned in paragraph (a)(ii) of subsection (1), as a reference to a constable of that force.

(5) For the purposes of section 2 any premises occupied for the purposes of a police force are to be treated as occupied by that force.

(6) For the purposes of sections 2 to 7 anything that would be regarded as done by a police force if the force were a body corporate is to be so regarded.

(7) Where—

   (a) by virtue of subsection (3) a person is treated for the purposes of section 2 as employed by a police force, and
   (b) by virtue of any other statutory provision (whenever made) he is, or is treated as, employed by another organisation,

the person is to be treated for those purposes as employed by both the force and the other organisation.

GENERAL COMMENTARY

Subsection (1)   **13.02**

    Section 3 of the Police (Scotland) Act 1967 provides that a police force shall consist of a Chief Constable, Regular Constables and Special Constables. A Regular Constable means a constable, including a Probationary Constable, to whom both pay and allowances are, by virtue of s.26 of the 1967 Act, payable and a Special Constable is a constable to whom allowances only are payable.

13.03 *Subsection (2)*

A police force is to be treated as owing duties of care as if it were a body corporate. Accordingly, a police force is to be treated as a separate legal entity. Any prosecution will be brought in the name of the relevant police force rather than the Chief Constable.

13.04 *Subsection (5)*

Any buildings occupied "for the purposes of" a police force are to be treated as occupied by the police force for the purposes of s.2(1)(b) (a duty owed as an occupier of premises).

Application to partnerships

14.01   **14.**—(1) For the purposes of this Act a partnership is to be treated as owing whatever duties of care it would owe if it were a body corporate.

(2) Proceedings for an offence under this Act alleged to have been committed by a partnership are to be brought in the name of the partnership (and not in that of any of its members).

(3) A fine imposed on a partnership on its conviction of an offence under this Act is to be paid out of the funds of the partnership.

(4) This section does not apply to a partnership that is a legal person under the law by which it is governed.

DEFINITIONS

14.02   Section 25: "Partnership" means:

(a) A partnership within the Partnership Act 1890; or
(b) A limited partnership registered under the Limited Partnerships Act 1907; or
(c) A firm or entity of similar character formed under the law of a country or territory outside the United Kingdom.

GENERAL COMMENTARY

14.03   This section does not apply to a partnership constituted under Scots Law (s.14(4)).

In Scotland a partnership is, "a legal person distinct from the partners of whom it is composed, but an individual partner may be charged on a decree or diligence directed against the firm, and on payment of the debts is entitled to relief pro rata from the firm and its other members" (The Partnership Act 1890, s.4(2)).

English law does not at present recognise a partnership as a separate legal entity. For the purposes of the Act, s.14 means that a partnership under English law is treated in a similar way to a body corporate with proceedings being brought in the name of the partnership, rather than the individual partners and with any fine being paid from partnership funds.

Section 14(3) states that the fine "is to be paid" out of partnership funds rather than "may be paid". This suggests that, under s.14, the individual partners would have no personal liability for any fine imposed on the partnership in the event that it could not be met from partnership funds. If that is correct it creates a protection for partners in English firms which is not available in Scotland. Section 14(3) does not apply to Scots partnerships and consequently the partners of Scots firms may be liable personally for such a debt (see s.4(2) of the 1890 Act, above).[13]

14.04 *Limited Liability Partnerships*

A limited liability partnership constituted in terms of the Limited Liability Partnerships Act 2000 is a body corporate, s.1(2).

14.05 *Foreign Partnerships*

Whether or not s.14 applies to a foreign partnership will depend upon the law of the country under which the partnership has been formed.

---

[13]   See the Joint Report of the Law Commission (No.283) and the Scottish Law Commission (No.192) on proposals for a new Partnerships Act, under which partnerships in England and Wales would become legal entities.

Procedure, evidence and sentencing

15.—(1) Any statutory provision (whenever made) about criminal pro- **15.01**
ceedings applies, subject to any prescribed adaptations or modifications, in
relation to proceedings under this Act against—
  (a) a department or other body listed in Schedule 1,
  (b) a police force,
  (c) a partnership,
  (d) a trade union, or
  (e) an employers' association that is not a corporation
as it applies in relation to proceedings against a corporation.
  (2) In this section—
"prescribed" means prescribed by an order made by the Secretary of
    State;
"provision about criminal proceedings" includes—
    (a) provision about procedure in or in connection with criminal
      proceedings;
    (b) provision about evidence in such proceedings;
    (c) provision about sentencing, or otherwise dealing with, persons
      convicted of offences;
"statutory" means contained in, or in an instrument made under, any Act
    or any Northern Ireland legislation.
  (3) A reference in this section to proceedings is to proceedings in England
and Wales or Northern Ireland.
  (4) An order under this section is subject to negative resolution procedure.

GENERAL NOTE
This section applies to proceedings in England and Wales or Northern Ireland only (subs.(3)). **15.02**
The High Court of Justiciary retains the power to create rules regulating criminal procedure in
Scotland which are introduced by Act of Adjournal.

Transfer of functions

16.—(1) This section applies where— **16.01**
  (a) a person's death has occurred, or is alleged to have occurred, in
    connection with the carrying out of functions by a relevant public
    organisation, and
  (b) subsequently there is a transfer of those functions, with the result
    that they are still carried out but no longer by that organisation.
  (2) In this section "relevant public organisation" means—
  (a) a department or other body listed in Schedule 1;
  (b) a corporation that is a servant or agent of the Crown;
  (c) a police force.
  (3) Any proceedings instituted against a relevant public organisation after
the transfer for an offence under this Act in respect of the person's death are
to be instituted against—
  (a) the relevant public organisation, if any, by which the functions
    mentioned in subsection (1) are currently carried out;
  (b) if no such organisation currently carries out the functions, the rele-
    vant public organisation by which the functions were last carried out.
This is subject to subsection (4).
  (4) If an order made by the Secretary of State so provides in relation to a
particular transfer of functions, the proceedings referred to in subsection (3)

may be instituted, or (if they have already been instituted) may be continued, against—
    (a) the organisation mentioned in subsection (1), or
    (b) such relevant public organisation (other than the one mentioned in subsection (1) or the one mentioned in subsection (3)(a) or (b)) as may be specified in the order.
    (5) If the transfer occurs while proceedings for an offence under this Act in respect of the person's death are in progress against a relevant public organisation, the proceedings are to be continued against—
    (a) the relevant public organisation, if any, by which the functions mentioned in subsection (1) are carried out as a result of the transfer;
    (b) if as a result of the transfer no such organisation carries out the functions, the same organisation as before.
This is subject to subsection (6).
    (6) If an order made by the Secretary of State so provides in relation to a particular transfer of functions, the proceedings referred to in subsection (5) may be continued against—
    (a) the organisation mentioned in subsection (1), or
    (b) such relevant public organisation (other than the one mentioned in subsection (1) or the one mentioned in subsection (5)(a) or (b)) as may be specified in the order.
    (7) An order under subsection (4) or (6) is subject to negative resolution procedure.

16.02 DEFINITIONS
"police force": s.13(1)
"corporation": s.25

16.03 GENERAL NOTE
This section applies to those cases involving "a relevant public organisation" as defined by s.16(2), where a person's death is alleged to have occurred in connection with the carrying out of functions by a relevant public organisation. In the cases in which there is a transfer of those functions with the result that they are still carried out but no longer by that organisation, subss.(3) and (4) direct against which organisation proceedings should be brought where the transfer has occurred subsequent to the person's death but prior to the commencement of proceedings. Subsections (5) and (6) deal with the position where the transfer occurs while proceedings for an offence under this Act in respect of the person's death have already commenced against a relevant public organisation.

DPP's consent required for proceedings

17.01 17.—Proceedings for an offence of corporate manslaughter—
    (a) may not be instituted in England and Wales without the consent of the Director of Public Prosecutions;
    (b) may not be instituted in Northern Ireland without the consent of the Director of Public Prosecutions for Northern Ireland.

17.02 GENERAL NOTE
This section applies to proceedings in England, Wales and Northern Ireland only.

No individual liability

18.01 18.—(1) An individual cannot be guilty of aiding, abetting, counselling or procuring the commission of an offence of corporate manslaughter.
    (2) An individual cannot be guilty of aiding, abetting, counselling or procuring, or being art and part in, the commission of an offence of corporate homicide.

No individual liability

GENERAL NOTE

18.02 This section, which excludes liability of an individual for an offence of corporate manslaughter or corporate homicide, represents one of the most contentious aspects of the Act and has been the subject of considerable debate and controversy since it was first recommended by the Law Commission in 1996. Subsection (1) applies to proceedings in England, Wales and Northern Ireland only and subs.(2) to Scotland only. Both subsections reflect the view expressed by the Law Commission in its report on Involuntary Manslaughter, in which it stated:

> "We intend that no individual should be liable to prosecution for the corporate offence, even as a secondary party. Our aim is... that the offence of killing by gross carelessness should be adapted so as to fit the special case of a corporation whose management or organisation of its activities is one of the causes of a death. The indirect extension of an individual's liability, by means of the new corporate offence, would be entirely contrary to our purpose..." (Law Com. No.237, 1996, para.8.58)

18.03 The report was one of a number produced by the Law Commission as part of a major project to codify the criminal law in England. The report on Involuntary Manslaughter, and in particular its recommendations in relation to corporate manslaughter, was very well received at the time by trade unions and health and safety pressure groups. Following its election victory in 1997, the New Labour government committed itself to legislating in relation to the offence of "corporate killing" and, although the government appeared initially to be attracted by the concept of secondary liability for individuals (see Home Office consultation paper, *Reforming the law on involuntary manslaughter: the Government's proposals*, May 2000), by the time the draft Bill was laid before parliament in 2005, government thinking reflected the views of the Law Commission expressed almost a decade before. In its introduction to the draft Bill the government stated its position in the following terms:

> "We are clear that the need for reform arises from the law operating in a restricted way for holding organisations themselves to account for gross negligence leading to death. Our proposal to tackle this focuses on changing the way in which an offence of manslaughter applies to organisations, and this is a matter of corporate not individual liability. We do not therefore intend to pursue new sanctions for individuals or to provide secondary liability." (Cm. 6497, March 2005, para.47.)

18.04 The draft Bill was subject to pre-legislative scrutiny by the Home Affairs and Work and Pensions Committee ("the HAWPC"), which submitted a report in December 2005[14] and the Corporate Homicide Expert Group ("the CHEG"), set up by the Scottish Executive in April 2005, whose remit was, "to review the law in Scotland on corporate liability for culpable homicide and to submit a report ... taking into account the proposals recently published by the Home Secretary". Both the HAWPC and the CHEG reached a similar conclusion, recommending that secondary liability should apply to an individual. The CHEG stated that secondary liability should apply where "...the prosecution could also prove that an individual director/senior officer's actions were a significant contributory factor to the death of the employee or member of the public"[15]. However, the government resisted moves to include individuals within the ambit of corporate manslaughter or homicide and the Bill presented before the House of Commons in July 2006 specifically excluded individual liability (Bill 220, cl.17).[16]

Liability of individuals at common law and by virtue of s.37(1) of HSWA **18.05**

Although an individual cannot be convicted of the statutory offence of corporate homicide, it would remain open to the prosecution to indict an individual in respect of culpable homicide if the facts warranted it. Equally, if an organisation is convicted of an offence under either s.2 or s.3 of the HSWA and the offence is "proved to have been committed with the consent or connivance of, or to have been attributable to any neglect on the part of, any director, manager,

---

[14] HC 540 Vols I–III, *http://www.publications.parliament.uk/pa/cm200506/cmselect/cmhaff/540/54002.htm* [Accessed February 26, 2008].
[15] The Scottish Government, *Corporate Homicide: Expert Group Report 2005*, para.12.5, *http://www.scotland.gov.uk/Publications/2005/11/14133559/35592* [Accessed February 26, 2008].
[16] For a more detailed analysis see House of Commons Library, *The Corporate Manslaughter and Corporate Homicide Bill*, Research Paper 06/46, *http://www.parliament.uk/commons/lib/research/rp2006/rp06-046.pdf* [Accessed February 26, 2008].

secretary or other similar officer of the body corporate or a person who was purporting to act in any such capacity, he as well as the body corporate shall be guilty of that offence and shall be liable to be proceeded against and punished accordingly" (HSWA, s.37(1)).

Prosecutions under s.37(1) have been rare in recent years, in part because of a perception that proof of subjective knowledge on the part of the director was necessary in order to establish guilt. It will be interesting to see whether the recent decision of the Appeal Court in England in *R v P Ltd*, [2007] W.L.R. (D.) 196 reverses the trend. In that case, it had been held at a preliminary hearing that subjective knowledge by the director was required of the material facts giving rise to the offence by the body corporate. On appeal it was held that an offence committed by a body corporate under the HSWA was attributable to neglect by an officer of that body, thereby amounting to an offence by that officer under s.37(1), if the officer either knew of the relevant facts giving rise to the health and safety offence or, if he did not know, should by reason of the circumstances have been put on inquiry as to whether the relevant safety procedures were in place. See also *Wotherspoon v HMA*, 1978 J.C. 74.

18.06 Insofar as sentencing is concerned, an individual potentially faces a substantial sentence of imprisonment for an offence of culpable homicide and an unlimited fine if convicted under s.37(1) of the HSWA as described above. Furthermore, a director could also face disqualification from acting as a director for a period up to 15 years (Company Directors Disqualifications Act 1986, s.2(1)).

18.07 A recent report, commissioned by the HSE and published in 2005, *A Survey of the use and effectiveness of the Company Directors Disqualification Act 1986 as a legal sanction against directors convicted of health and safety offences*, found that this power is exercised very rarely in relation to health and safety offences (approximately 10 times between 1986 and 2005), noting that, "interviews conducted with HSE operations directors and their counterparts in local authorities indicate a surprisingly low level of awareness of the 1986 Act provisions, and their utilisation in practice. Undoubtedly, the use of the disqualification sanction has not enjoyed a high priority by prosecutors—at least at a formal recorded level." In response to the report, in May 2006 the Health and Safety Commission issued instructions to all inspectors to seek greater use by the courts of director disqualification as a penalty. It remains to be seen whether the introduction of the Act coupled with the HSE drive to increase awareness of the powers to disqualify directors will result in this power being exercised more frequently in the future by the courts.

Convictions under this Act and under health and safety legislation

19.01 **19.**—(1) Where in the same proceedings there is—
(a) a charge of corporate manslaughter or corporate homicide arising out of a particular circumstances, and
(b) a charge against the same defendant of a health and safety offence arising out of the same circumstances,
the jury may, if the interests of justice so require, be invited to return a verdict on each charge.

(2) An organisation that has been convicted of corporate manslaughter or corporate homicide arising out of a particular set of circumstances may, if the interests of justice so require, be charged with a health and safety offence arising out of some or all of those circumstances.

(3) In this section "health and safety offence" means an offence under any health and safety legislation.

GENERAL NOTE
19.02 Section 19(1) provides that, where, in the same proceedings, an organisation faces charges of corporate homicide and health and safety offences arising out of the same circumstances, the jury may, if the interests of justice so require, be invited to return a verdict on each charge. An example of where this may arise would be where an organisation and a director of that organisation appeared on the same indictment—the former in respect of charges under the CMCHA and the HSWA, and the latter in respect of a charge under s.37(1) of the HSWA. A jury would not be able, if it wished to do so, to return a verdict of guilty in respect of the charge under s.37(1) if it had not also returned a verdict of guilty in respect of the HSWA charge against the organisation. Subsection (2) seeks to achieve the same result in circumstances where the organisation was initially indicted in respect of an offence under the CMCHA only.

It should be noted that the view of the HSE is that, "although most commonly there will be criminal proceedings against the company as well as against the director or manager, it is not necessary to prosecute both. Section 37 does not require a conviction of the body corporate, but does requires proof that it has committed an offence" (see HSE, *Enforcement Guide, (England and Wales)*). Support for this position may be found in a first instance case, *R v Mather & others* (2001) September 19, Leeds Crown Court (unreported). (For a discussion of that case see the *Health and Safety Bulletin*, issue 303, LexisNexis, November 2001).

Abolition of liability of corporations for manslaughter at common law

20.—The common law offence of manslaughter by gross negligence is **20.01** abolished in its application to corporations, and in any application it has to other organisations to which section 1 applies.

GENERAL NOTE
This section does not apply to proceedings in Scotland. It was held in *Transco plc v HM* **20.02** *Advocate*, 2004 S.L.T. 41, the only case in which a corporate body has been indicted in Scotland in respect of a charge of culpable homicide, that such a charge can competently be brought against a corporate body. However, in that case, a plea to the relevancy was upheld. Having regard to the fundamental difficulties encountered by the Crown, both in Scotland and England, in successfully prosecuting corporate bodies in respect of offences of corporate homicide/manslaughter (difficulties which the CMCHA is intended to overcome), it is likely that prosecutions against corporate bodies in respect of culpable homicide in Scotland will remain extremely rare.

General and supplemental

Power to extend section 1 to other organisations

21.—(1) The Secretary of State may by order amend section 1 so as to **21.01** extend the categories of organisation to which that section applies.
(2) An order under this section may make any amendment to this Act that is incidental or supplemental to, or consequential on, an amendment made by virtue of subsection (1).
(3) An order under this section is subject to affirmative resolution procedure.

Power to amend Schedule 1

22.—(1) The Secretary of State may amend Schedule 1 by order. **22.01**
(2) A statutory instrument containing an order under this section is subject to affirmative resolution procedure, unless the only amendments to Schedule 1 that it makes are amendments within subsection (3).
In that case the instrument is subject to negative resolution procedure.
(3) An amendment is within this subsection if—
(a) it is consequential on a department or other body listed in Schedule 1 changing its name,
(b) in the case of an amendment adding a department or other body to Schedule 1, it is consequential on the transfer to the department or other body of functions all of which were previously exercisable by one or more organisations to which section 1 applies, or
(c) in the case of an amendment removing a department or other body from Schedule 1, it is consequential on—
(i) the abolition of the department or other body, or
(ii) the transfer of all the functions of the department or other body to one or more organisations to which section 1 applies.

Power to extend section 2(2)

23.01 **23.**—(1) The Secretary of State may by order amend section 2(2) to make it include any category of person (not already included) who—
(a) is required by virtue of a statutory provision to remain or reside on particular premises, or
(b) is otherwise subject to a restriction of his liberty.
(2) An order under this section may make any amendment to this Act that is incidental or supplemental to, or consequential on, an amendment made by virtue of subsection (1).
(3) An order under this section is subject to affirmative resolution procedure.

Orders

24.01 **24.**—(1) A power of the Secretary of State to make an order under this Act is exercisable by statutory instrument.
(2) Where an order under this Act is subject to "negative resolution procedure" the statutory instrument containing the order is subject to annulment in pursuance of a resolution of either House of Parliament.
(3) Where an order under this Act is subject to "affirmative resolution procedure" the order may not be made unless a draft has been laid before, and approved by a resolution of, each House of Parliament.
(4) An order under this Act—
(a) may make different provision for different purposes;
(b) may make transitional or saving provision.

Interpretation

25.01 **25.**—In this Act—
"armed forces" has the meaning given by section 12(1);
"corporation" does not include a corporation sole but includes any body corporate wherever incorporated;
"employee" means an individual who works under a contract of employment or apprenticeship (whether express or implied and, if express, whether oral or in writing), and related expressions are to be construed accordingly; see also sections 11(3)(a), 12(2) and 13(3) (which apply for the purposes of section 2);
"employers' association" has the meaning given by section 122 of the Trade Union and Labour Relations (Consolidation) Act 1992 (c. 52) or Article 4 of the Industrial Relations (Northern Ireland) Order 1992 (S.I. 1992/807 (N.I. 5));
"enforcement authority" means an authority responsible for the enforcement of any health and safety legislation;
"health and safety legislation" means any statutory provision dealing with health and safety matters, including in particular provision contained in the Health and Safety at Work etc. Act 1974 (c. 37) or the Health and Safety at Work (Northern Ireland) Order 1978 (S.I. 1978/1039 (N.I. 9));
"member", in relation to the armed forces, is to be read in accordance with section 12(3);
"partnership" means—
(a) a partnership within the Partnership Act 1890 (c. 39), or
(b) a limited partnership registered under the Limited Partnerships Act 1907 (c. 24),

or a firm or entity of a similar character formed under the law of a
country or territory outside the United Kingdom;
"police force" has the meaning given by section 13(1);
"premises" includes land, buildings and moveable structures;
"public authority" has the same meaning as in section 6 of the Human
Rights Act 1998 (c. 42) (disregarding subsections (3)(a) and (4) of
that section);
"publicity order" means an order under section 10(1);
"remedial order" means an order under section 9(1);
"statutory provision", except in section 15, means provision contained in,
or in an instrument made under, any Act, any Act of the Scottish
Parliament or any Northern Ireland legislation;
"trade union" has the meaning given by section 1 of the Trade Union and
Labour Relations (Consolidation) Act 1992 (c. 52) or Article 3 of the
Industrial Relations (Northern Ireland) Order 1992 (S.I. 1992/807
(N.I. 5)).

Minor and consequential amendments

26.—Schedule 2 (minor and consequential amendments) has effect. **26.01**

Commencement and savings

27.—(1) The preceding provisions of this Act come into force in accor- **27.01**
dance with provision made by order of the Secretary of State.

(2) An order bringing into force paragraph (d) of section 2(1) is subject to
affirmative resolution procedure.

(3) Section 1 does not apply in relation to anything done or omitted
before the commencement of that section.

(4) Section 20 does not affect any liability, investigation, legal proceeding
or penalty for or in respect of an offence committed wholly or partly before
the commencement of that section.

(5) For the purposes of subsection (4) an offence is committed wholly or
partly before the commencement of section 20 if any of the conduct or
events alleged to constitute the offence occurred before that commencement.

Extent and territorial application

28.—(1) Subject to subsection (2), this Act extends to England and Wales, **28.01**
Scotland and Northern Ireland.

(2) An amendment made by this Act extends to the same part or parts of
the United Kingdom as the provision to which it relates.

(3) Section 1 applies if the harm resulting in death is sustained in the
United Kingdom or—

(a) within the seaward limits of the territorial sea adjacent to the United
Kingdom;

(b) on a ship registered under Part 2 of the Merchant Shipping Act 1995
(c.21);

(c) on a British-controlled aircraft as defined in section 92 of the Civil
Aviation Act 1982 (c.16);

(d) on a British-controlled hovercraft within the meaning of that section
as applied in relation to hovercraft by virtue of provision made under
the Hovercraft Act 1968 (c.59);

(e) in any place to which an Order in Council under section 10(1) of the

Petroleum Act 1998 (c.17) applies (criminal jurisdiction in relation to offshore activities).

(4) For the purposes of subsection 3(b) to (d) harm sustained on a ship, aircraft or hovercraft includes harm sustained by a person who—

(a) is then no longer on board the ship, aircraft or hovercraft in consequence of the wrecking of it or of some other mishap affecting it or occurring on it, and

(b) sustains the harm in consequence of that event.

DEFINITIONS

28.02   "ship": s.313 Merchant Shipping Act 1995
"British-controlled aircraft": s.92, Civil Aviation Act 1982 (c.16)
"British-controlled hovercraft": s.4(1) Hovercraft Act 1968

GENERAL NOTE

28.03   The Act applies in relation to any death caused by harm sustained anywhere in the UK.

28.04   *Subsection (3) "harm resulting in death"*
The Ministry of Justice guide provides that this "typically" applies where there has been a physical injury which is fatal. Whilst in general the injury and death will occur in close proximity, the guide suggests that there may be instances where the harm is sustained in the UK and death occurs abroad. One example would be an accident on a British ship where the injured party is taken to hospital in a foreign port and dies there. In such cases the UK courts would have jurisdiction.
The use of the word "typically" in the guide suggests that there may be instances where the harm is not a physical injury, for example psychological injury, such as Post-Traumatic Stress Disorder, or workplace stress.

28.05   *Subsection (3)(a) within the area of UK territorial Sea*
The current limits of the UK territorial sea are defined in the Territorial Sea Act 1987, which extended the relevant area to a distance of 12 nautical miles.

28.06   *Subsection (3)(b) on a British ship*
If the harmful act or omission occurs on a ship registered under Pt 2 of the Merchant Shipping Act 1995, the Act applies whether or not the ship is within UK territorial waters. Ships registered under Pt 2 of the 1995 Act are registered in the UK Shipping Register, administered by the Maritime and Coastguard Agency ("the MCA").

28.07   *Subsection (3)(c) on a British controlled Aircraft*
Section 92, Civil Aviation Act 1982:

"British-controlled aircraft" means an aircraft—

(a) which is for the time being registered in the United Kingdom; or

(b) which is not for the time being registered in any country but in the case of which either the operator of the aircraft or each person entitled as owner to any legal or beneficial interest in it satisfies the following requirements, namely—

(i) that he is a person qualified to be the owner of a legal or beneficial interest in an aircraft registered in the United Kingdom; and

(ii) that he resides or has his principal place of business in the United Kingdom; or

(c) which, being for the time being registered in some other country, is for the time being chartered by demise to a person who, or to persons each of whom, satisfies the requirements aforesaid;" (Civil Aviation Act 1982, C16, Pt IV, s.92.)

28.08   *Subsection (3)(d) on a British controlled hovercraft*
"Hovercraft" means "a vehicle which is designed to be supported when in motion wholly or partly by air expelled from the vehicle to form a cushion of which the boundaries include the ground, water or other surface beneath the vehicle" (Hovercraft Act 1968, s.4(1)).

Subsection (3)(e) on, under or above an Offshore Installation   **28.09**

The offence is extended to any place to which criminal jurisdiction has been extended by an order under s.10(1) of the Petroleum Act 1998.

The Criminal Jurisdiction (Offshore Activities) Order 1987 was issued under the powers contained in s.22 of the Oil and Gas Enterprise Act 1982, which is now superseded by the 1998 Act. The 1987 Order provides that:

> "[A]ny act or omission which—
>> (a) takes place on, under or above an installation in waters to which this Order applies or any waters within 500 metres of any such installation: and
>> (b) would, if taking place in any part of the United Kingdom, constitute an offence under the law in force in that part,
> shall be treated for the purposes of that law as taking place in that part." (Criminal Jurisdiction (Offshore Activities) Order 1987, Art.3.)

"Installation" is not defined in the Order other than to say it includes "an installation in transit". There is a definition in the 1998 Act, "any floating structure or device maintained on a station by whatever means" (s.13). That would, at first reading, appear to preclude an installation in transit as it is not "on station" although s.10(10) states expressly that the section does apply to "installations notwithstanding that they are for the time being in transit". For the two provisions to make sense the words "which is capable of being" require to be inserted before "maintained" in the definition in s.13. The definition may also extend beyond oil rigs to include sub-sea devices and consequently to acts or omissions occurring within 500m of such devices. Wind farms and other renewable energy installations[17] are expressly excluded by s.10(10),[18] although s.85 of the Energy Act 2004 provides for an Order in Council, which could apply the provisions of the 2007 Act to such installations as part of general criminal law.[19]

Section 10 (4) of the 1998 Act provides that where a body corporate is guilty of an offence   **28.10**
"and that offence is proved to have been committed with the consent or connivance of, or attributable to any neglect on the part of, any director, manager, secretary or other similar officer of the body corporate or any person who was purporting to act in any such capacity, he as well as the body corporate shall be guilty of that offence and shall be liable to be proceeded against and punished accordingly".

Does this allow prosecution of individuals for corporate homicide? Section 10(4) appears to provide that where a body corporate is guilty of the offence of corporate homicide an individual director, manager or similar officer, may be held similarly liable for that offence. This is contrary to the expressly stated intention of the CMCHA. Section 18 of the Act states that "an individual cannot be guilty of aiding, abetting, counselling or procuring, or being art and part in, the commission of" an offence of corporate manslaughter or corporate homicide. That exclusion would not necessarily prevent an individual from being held liable by such an express statutory provision.

The territorial limits of the area to which the 1987 Order applies are the territorial waters of   **28.11**
the United Kingdom (see above) and any areas designated by orders made under s.1(7) of the Continental Shelf Act 1964 (the "UKCS"). The current limits of the UKCS are defined by the Continental Shelf (Designation of Areas) Consolidation Order 2000 (SI 3062/2000) and the Continental Shelf (Designation of Areas) Order 2001 (SI 3670/2001).[20] Section 10(8) of the 1998 Act permits an Order in Council extending jurisdiction to a foreign sector of the Continental Shelf where it forms part of a cross boundary field part of which is within the area of the UKCS or territorial sea.

The effect of the 1998 Act and the 1987 Order is to provide for concurrent jurisdiction in   **28.12**
every part of the United Kingdom (s.10(6)). Whilst this would allow for a breach of the Act to

---

[17]   Defined in s.104 of the Energy Act 2004.

[18]   A former oil and gas installation in the Beatrice Field is currently being operated as a wind farm and, accordingly, would appear now to be excluded by s.10(10).

[19]   Section 85 of the Energy Act 2004 provides that an Order in Council may provide that acts or omissions occurring on, under or above a renewable energy installation and which would constitute an offence if occurring in a part of the UK are to be treated as taking place in that part. Relevant waters for this purpose are UK territorial waters and waters in the Renewable Energy Zone (see The Renewable Energy Zone (Designation of Area) Order 2004 or *www.ukho.gov.uk*, under Law of the Sea, UK Limits, for a map [accessed February 26, 2008]).

[20]   See *www.ukho.gov.uk*, under Law of the Sea, UK Limits, for a map illustrating the UKCS area [accessed February 26, 2008].

be prosecuted in any court in the United Kingdom, in practice offences occurring on installations in the Scottish sector are likely to be prosecuted in the High Court of Justiciary and those in the Southern sector in the appropriate courts in England. The United Kingdom Offshore Oil and Gas Industry Association, Oil and Gas UK, has entered into arrangements agreeing that Grampian Police exercise jurisdiction over all installations in the Scottish sector (above 55° to 50° north). Norfolk and Humberside Constabulary have jurisdiction in the Southern sector, with Merseyside Police covering Liverpool Bay and Lancashire Police covering Morecambe Bay (HSE Operations Notice 3, *Liaison with other bodies*, May, 2007).

28.13 *Consent of the Scottish Parliament*

The consent of the Scottish Parliament is to be sought in relation to any amendments related to devolved matters. Devolved matters are those within the legislative competence of the Scottish Parliament, that is not reserved by Westminster (see s.29 and Sch.5 of the Scotland Act 1998 for further details). Health and safety and the application of Scots law to offshore activities are both specifically reserved matters (Sch.5, ss.H2 and D2). A provision modifying Scots criminal law, as it applies to any reserved matter, is to be treated as relating to a reserved matter and therefore outside the competence of the Scottish Parliament (s.29(4)).

Short title

29.01   29.—This Act may be cited as the Corporate Manslaughter and Corporate Homicide Act 2007.

Schedule 1

SCHEDULES

SCHEDULE 1   Section 1

LIST OF GOVERNMENT DEPARTMENTS ETC

Assets Recovery Agency   **30.01**
Attorney General's Office
Cabinet Office
Central Office of Information
Crown Office and Procurator Fiscal Service
Crown Prosecution Service
Department for Communities and Local Government
Department for Constitutional Affairs (including the Scotland Office and the Wales Office)
Department for Culture, Media and Sport
Department for Education and Skills
Department for Environment, Food and Rural Affairs
Department for International Development
Department for Transport
Department for Work and Pensions
Department of Health
Department of Trade and Industry
Export Credits Guarantee Department
Foreign and Commonwealth Office
Forestry Commission
General Register Office for Scotland
Government Actuary's Department
Her Majesty's Land Registry
Her Majesty's Revenue and Customs
Her Majesty's Treasury
Home Office
Ministry of Defence
National Archives
National Archives of Scotland
National Audit Office
National Savings and Investments
National School of Government
Northern Ireland Audit Office
Northern Ireland Court Service
Northern Ireland Office
Office for National Statistics
Office of the Deputy Prime Minister
Office of Her Majesty's Chief Inspector of Education and Training in Wales
Ordnance Survey
Privy Council Office
Public Prosecution Service for Northern Ireland
Registers of Scotland Executive Agency
Revenue and Customs Prosecutions Office
Royal Mint
Scottish Executive
Serious Fraud Office
Treasury Solicitor's Department
UK Trade and Investment
Welsh Assembly Government

SCHEDULE 2   Section 26

MINOR AND CONSEQUENTIAL AMENDMENTS

31.01 *Coroners Act 1988 (c. 13)*

1 (1) The Coroners Act 1988 is amended as follows.

(2) In the following provisions, after "manslaughter" there is inserted ", corporate manslaughter"—

(a) section 11(6) (no finding of guilt at coroner's inquest) (twice);

(b) subsection (1)(a)(i) of section 16 (adjournment of inquest in event of criminal proceedings);

(c) subsections (1)(a) and (2)(a) of section 17 (coroner to be informed of result of criminal proceedings).

(3) In section 35(1) (interpretation), after the definition of "Greater London" there is inserted—

  " "person", in relation to an offence of corporate manslaughter, includes organisation;".

Criminal Justice Act 2003 (c. 44)

2 In Schedule 4 to the Criminal Justice Act 2003 (qualifying offences for purposes of section 62), after paragraph 4 there is inserted—

  "Corporate manslaughter

  4A An offence under section 1 of the Corporate Manslaughter and Corporate Homicide Act 2007."

3 (1) Schedule 5 to that Act (qualifying offences for purposes of Part 10) is amended as follows.

(2) After paragraph 4 there is inserted—

  "Corporate manslaughter

  4A An offence under section 1 of the Corporate Manslaughter and Corporate Homicide Act 2007."

(3) After paragraph 33 there is inserted—

  "Corporate manslaughter

  33A An offence under section 1 of the Corporate Manslaughter and Corporate Homicide Act 2007."

Criminal Justice (Northern Ireland) Order 2004 (S.I. 2004/1500 (N.I. 9))

4 In Schedule 2 to the Criminal Justice (Northern Ireland) Order 2004 (qualifying offences for purposes of Article 21), after paragraph 4 there is inserted—

  "Corporate manslaughter

  4A An offence under section 1 of the Corporate Manslaughter and Corporate Homicide Act 2007."

APPENDIX 1

These notes refer to the Corporate Manslaughter and Corporate Homicide Act 2007 (c.19) which received Royal Assent on 26 July 2007

CORPORATE MANSLAUGHTER AND CORPORATE HOMICIDE ACT 2007 EXPLANATORY NOTES

INTRODUCTION

1.   These explanatory notes relate to the Corporate Manslaughter and Corporate Homicide Act which received Royal Assent on 26 July 2007. They have been prepared by the Ministry of Justice in order to assist the reader in understanding the Act. They do not form part of the Act and have not been endorsed by Parliament.

2.   The notes need to be read in conjunction with the Act. They are not, and are not meant to be, a comprehensive description of the Act. So where a section or part of a section does not seem to require any explanation or comment, none is given.

SUMMARY

3.   The Act makes provision for a new offence of corporate manslaughter (to be called corporate homicide in Scotland) and for this to apply to companies and other incorporated bodies, Government departments and similar bodies, police forces and certain unincorporated associations. The Act has 29 sections and 2 Schedules.

4.   Section 1 defines the offence and identifies the sorts of organisation to which it will apply. The effect of sections 2 to 7 is to identify the sort of activities covered by the new offence, and to specify certain functions performed by public authorities in relation to which the offence will not apply. Section 8 outlines factors for the jury to consider when assessing an organisation's culpability. Sections 9 and 10 make provision for remedial orders and publicity orders to be made on conviction.

5.   Sections 11 to 13 deal with the application of the offence to the Crown and police forces, where a number of provisions are required to reflect the particular status of Crown bodies and police forces. Section 14 makes provision to accommodate the application of the offence to partnerships. Section 15 makes further supplemental provision to ensure that rules of procedure, evidence and sentencing apply to Crown bodies, police forces and those unincorporated bodies to which the offence applies. Section 16 sets out where liability will fall following machinery of Government changes or other cases where functions are transferred.

6.   Sections 17 to 20 deal with a number of ancillary matters. These require the consent of the Director of Public Prosecutions to commence proceedings in England and Wales or Northern Ireland; preclude the prosecution of individuals as secondary participants in the new offence; clarify that convictions under this Act would not preclude conviction under health and safety legislation on the same facts; and abolish the common law offence of manslaughter by gross negligence in so far as it applies to

companies and other bodies that are liable to the new offence. Sections 21 to 23 provide powers to extend the offence to other types of organisation, to amend the list of Government departments and other bodies in Schedule 1 and to extend the forms of custody or detention that give rise to relevant duties of care. Sections 24 to 28 deal with general matters including extent and jurisdiction.

7.   The Schedules to the Act set out the Government departments and other similar bodies to which the offence will apply and make a number of minor and consequential amendments.

BACKGROUND

8.   Prior to this legislation it was possible for a corporate body, such as a company, to be prosecuted for a wide range of criminal offences, including manslaughter. To be guilty of the common law offence of gross negligence manslaughter, a company had to be in gross breach of a duty of care owed to the victim. The prosecution of a company for manslaughter by gross negligence was often referred to as "corporate manslaughter". As the law stood, before a company could be convicted of manslaughter, a "directing mind" of the organisation (that is, a senior individual who could be said to embody the company in his actions and decisions) also had to be guilty of the offence. This is known as the identification principle. Crown bodies (those organisations that are legally a part of the Crown, such as Government departments) could not be prosecuted for criminal offences under the doctrine of Crown immunity. In addition, many Crown bodies, such as Government departments, do not have a separate legal identity for the purposes of a prosecution.

9.   In 1996 the Law Commission's report "Legislating the Criminal Code: Involuntary Manslaughter" (Law Com 237) included proposals for a new offence of corporate killing that would act as a stand-alone provision for prosecuting companies to complement offences primarily aimed at individuals. The Law Commission's report, including its proposals on corporate killing, provided the basis for the Government's subsequent consultation paper in 2000 "Reforming the Law on Involuntary Manslaughter: the Government's Proposals". These papers, and a summary of responses to the consultation paper, are available on the Home Office website (*www.homeoffice.gov.uk*).

10.   A draft Corporate Manslaughter Bill (Cm 6497) was published in March 2005. This set out the Government's proposals for legislating for reform and proposed an offence based on the Law Commission's proposals, with some modifications, including the application of the new offence to Crown bodies. The draft Bill was subject to pre-legislative scrutiny by the Home Affairs and Work and Pensions Committees in the House of Commons that autumn. Their report was published in December 2005 (HC 540 I-III) and the Government responded in March 2006 (Cm 6755).

11.   Although Scots criminal law on culpable homicide differs from the law of manslaughter elsewhere in the UK, the same issues of identifying a directing mind have arisen in Scotland. In 2005 the Scottish Executive established an Expert Group to review the law in Scotland on corporate liability for culpable homicide. The Group reported on 17 November 2005 and the report and other papers are available on the Scottish Executive website (*www.scotland.gov.uk*).

TERRITORIAL EXTENT

12.   The Act extends to the whole of the UK. Some provisions are, by their nature, only relevant to some parts of the UK.

13.   The Act is essentially concerned with health and safety, which is not a devolved matter in Scotland.

COMMENTARY ON SECTIONS

Section 1: The offence

14.   *Section 1(1)* defines the new offence, which will be called corporate manslaughter in England and Wales and Northern Ireland and corporate homicide in Scotland. The new offence builds on key aspects of the common law offence of gross negligence manslaughter in England and Wales and Northern Ireland, described in paragraph 8 above. However, rather than being contingent on the guilt of one or more individuals, liability for the new offence depends on a finding of gross negligence in the way in which the activities of the organisation are run. In summary, the offence is committed where, in particular circumstances, an organisation owes a duty to take reasonable care for a person's safety and the way in which activities of the organisation have been managed or organised amounts to a gross breach of that duty and causes the person's death. How the activities were managed or organised by senior management must be a substantial element of the gross breach.

15.   The elements of the new offence are:

- The organisation must owe a "relevant duty of care" to the victim. The relevant duties of care are set out in section 2.

- The organisation must be in breach of that duty of care as a result of the way in which the activities of the organisation were managed or organised. This test is not linked to a particular level of management but considers how an activity was managed within the organisation as a whole. *Section 1(3)* stipulates that an organisation cannot be convicted of the offence unless a substantial element of the breach lies in the way the senior management of the organisation managed or organised its activities.

- The way in which the organisation's activities were managed or organised (referred to in these notes as "the management failure") must have caused the victim's death. The usual principles of causation in the criminal law will apply to determine this question. This means that the management failure need not have been the sole cause of death; it need only be a cause (although intervening acts may break the chain of causation in certain circumstances).

- The management failure must amount to a gross breach of the duty of care. *Section 1(4)(b)* sets out the test for whether a particular breach is "gross". The test asks whether the conduct that constitutes the breach falls far below what could reasonably have been expected. This reflects the threshold for the common law offence of gross negligence manslaughter. Section 8 sets out a number of factors for the jury to take into account when considering this issue. There is no question of liability where the management of an activity includes reasonable safeguards and a death nonetheless occurs.

16.   Section 1(2) sets out the sort of organisation to which the new offence applies. In the first place, this is corporations. These are defined as any body corporate, whether incorporated in the United Kingdom or elsewhere. This includes companies incorporated under companies legislation, as well as bodies incorporated under statute (as is the case with many non-Departmental Public Bodies and other bodies in the public sector) or by Royal Charter. However, the definition specifically excludes corporations sole, which cover a number of individual offices in England and Wales and Northern Ireland. Section 1(2) also applies the offence to partnerships, trade unions and employers' associations, if the organisation concerned is an employer. These bodies are defined in section 25. The definition of partnership

extends to partnerships covered by the Partnership Act 1890 and limited partnerships registered under the Limited Partnerships Act 1907 but not to limited liability partnerships created under the Limited Liability Partnerships Act 2000, which are bodies corporate and therefore organisations to which the offence applies by virtue of section 1(2)(a). The list of organisations to which the offence applies can be further extended by secondary legislation, for example to further types of unincorporated association, subject to the affirmative resolution procedure (section 21).

17.   The term "senior management" is defined in *section 1(4)* to mean those persons who play a significant role in the management of the whole or a substantial part of the organisation's activities. This covers both those in the direct chain of management as well as those in, for example, strategic or regulatory compliance roles.

18.   The Act also binds the Crown and will apply to a range of Crown bodies such as government departments. Crown bodies rarely have a separate legal personality. Where they do, the application of the offence to corporations (and the Act's application to the Crown) means that the offence will also apply to these bodies. Where they do not, a mechanism is required to identify which Crown bodies are covered by the offence and this is achieved by applying the offence to a list of government departments and other bodies set out in Schedule 1. Section 22 sets out the procedure for amending the Schedule.

19.   The new offence will be triable only in the Crown Court in England and Wales and Northern Ireland and the High Court of Justiciary in Scotland. These represent equivalent levels of court and involve proceedings before a jury. The sanction is an unlimited fine *(section 1(6))*, although the court will also be empowered to impose a remedial order *(section 9)* and a publicity order *(section 10)* on a convicted organisation.

Section 2: Meaning of "relevant duty of care"

20.   The new offence only applies in circumstances where an organisation owed a duty of care to the victim under the law of negligence. This reflects the position under the common law offence of gross negligence manslaughter and, by defining the necessary relationship between the defendant organisation and victim, sets out the broad scope of the offence. Duties of care commonly owed by corporations include the duty owed by an employer to his employees to provide a safe system of work and by an occupier of buildings and land to people in or on, or potentially affected by, the property. Duties of care also arise out of the activities that are conducted by corporations, such as the duty owed by transport companies to their passengers.

21.   *Section 2(1)* requires the duty of care to be one that is owed under the law of negligence. This will commonly be a duty owed at common law, although in certain circumstances these duties have been superseded by statutory provision. For example, in the case of the duty owed by an occupier, duties are now owed under the Occupiers' Liability Acts 1957 and 1984 and the Defective Premises Act 1972 (and equivalent legislation in Northern Ireland and Scotland), although the common law continues to define by whom and to whom the duty is owed. In some circumstances, liability in the law of negligence has been superseded by statutory provision imposing strict liability, for example, the liability of carriers is governed by the Carriage of Air Act 1961. *Section 2(4)* makes provision for the offence to apply in these circumstances too. The section also, in *subsection (6)*, makes it clear that the application of the offence is not affected by common law rules precluding liability in the law of negligence where people are jointly engaged in a criminal enterprise (an aspect of the rule referred to by the Latin maxim "ex turpi causa non oritur actio") or because a person has accepted a risk of harm ("volenti non fit injuria").

22.   Section 2(1) requires the duty of care to arise out of certain specific functions or activities performed by the organisation. The effect is that the offence will only apply where an organisation owes a duty of care:

- to its **employees or to other persons working for the organisation**. This will include an employer's duty to provide a safe system of work for its employees. An organisation may also owe duties of care to those whose work it is able to control or direct, even though they are not formally employed by it. This might include contractors, secondees, or volunteers. The new offence does not impose new duties of care where these are not currently owed. But where such duties are owed, breach of them can trigger the offence.

- as **occupier** of premises (which is defined to include land). This covers organisations' responsibilities to ensure, for example, that buildings they occupy are kept in a safe condition.

- when the organisation is **supplying goods or services**. This will include duties owed by organisations to their customers and will cover, for example, duties owed by transport providers to their passengers and by retailers for the safety of their products. It will also cover the supply of services by the public sector, for example, NHS bodies providing medical treatment.

- when **constructing or maintaining buildings, infrastructure or vehicles etc or when using plant or vehicles etc**. In many circumstances, duties of care owed, for example, to ensure that adequate safety precautions are taken when repairing a road or in maintaining the safety of vehicles etc will be duties owed by an organisation in relation to the supply of a service or because it is operating commercially. But that may not be apt to cover public sector bodies in all such circumstances. These categories ensure that no lacuna is left in this respect.

- when carrying out **other activities on a commercial basis**. This ensures that activities that are not the supply of goods and services but which are still performed by companies and others commercially, such as farming or mining, are covered by the offence.

- that is owed **because a person is being held in detention or custody**. Section 2(2) sets out various forms of custody or detention covered by this: being detained in a prison or similar establishment, in a custody area at a court or police station or in immigration detention facilities; being held or transported under immigration or prison escort arrangements; being placed in premises used to accommodate children and young people on a secure basis; and being detained under mental health legislation. The commencement of this part of the legislation requires the further approval of Parliament (see paragraph 66 below).

23.   The effect is, broadly, to include within the offence the sort of activities typically pursued by companies and other corporate bodies, whether performed by commercial organisations or by Crown or other public bodies. Many functions that are peculiarly an aspect of government are not covered by the offence because they will not fall within any of the categories of duty of care in this section. In particular, the offence will not extend to circumstances where public bodies perform activities for the benefit of the community at large but without supplying services to particular individuals. This includes wider policy-making activities on the part of central government, such as setting regulatory standards and issuing guidance to public bodies on the exercise of their functions. In many circumstances, duties of care are unlikely to be owed in respect of such activities in any event, and they will remain subject to other forms of public accountability. Sections 3 to 7 provide that the offence does not apply to the performance of specified public functions. However,

whether the offence is capable of applying in any given circumstances will depend in the first place on whether a duty of care is owed to a person by an organisation, and whether the duty of care is a "relevant duty of care" by reason of section 2.

24.   In criminal proceedings, questions of law are decided by the judge, whilst questions of fact, and the application of the law to the facts of the case, are generally for the jury, directed by the judge. *Section 2(5)* provides that the existence of a duty of care in a particular case is a matter of law for the judge to decide. This reflects the heavily legal nature of the tests relating to the existence of a duty of care in the law of negligence. Because the judge will be deciding whether the circumstances of the case give rise to a duty of care, he will need to make certain determinations of fact that are usually for the jury. For example, if considering whether a corporation owes a duty of care as employer, the judge will need to decide whether the victim was an employee of the corporation. The questions of fact that the judge will need to consider will generally be uncontroversial and in any event will only be decided by the judge for the purposes of the duty of care question. If they otherwise affect the case, they will be for the jury to decide.

Section 3: Public policy decisions, exclusively public functions and statutory inspections

25.   Section 3 makes provision specifically to exclude certain matters from the ambit of the offence. *Section 3(1)* deals with decisions of public policy taken by public authorities. (Public authorities are defined by reference to the Human Rights Act 1998 and include core public bodies such as Government departments and local government bodies, as well as any other body some of whose functions are of a public nature. Courts and tribunals, which are not covered by the new offence, are excluded.) At present, the law of negligence recognises that some decisions taken by public bodies are not justiciable, in other words, are not susceptible to review in the courts. This is because they involve decisions involving competing public priorities or other questions of public policy. This might, for example, include decisions by Primary Care Trusts about the funding of particular treatments. A recent example in which the courts declined to find a duty of care on this basis related to whether the Department of Health owed a duty of care to issue interim advice about the safety of a particular drug. In many circumstances, these sorts of issues will not arise in respect of matters covered by the specified categories of duty within section 2. And basing the offence on the duty of care should mean that the offence would not apply to these sorts of decision in any event. Section 3(1) confirms, however, that deaths alleged to have been caused by such decisions will not come within the scope of the offence.

26.   *Section 3(2)* provides for an exemption in respect of intrinsically public functions. In many circumstances, functions of this nature will not be covered by the categories of duty set out in section 2 (see paragraph 22 above). However, it is possible that some such functions will amount to the supply of goods or services or be performed commercially, particularly if performed by the private sector on behalf of the State. In other circumstances, things done in the exercise of such a function will involve the use of equipment or vehicles. Section 3(2) specifically provides that an organisation will not be liable for a breach of any duty of care owed in respect of things done in the exercise of "exclusively public functions", unless the organisation owes the duty in its capacity as an employer or as an occupier of premises. This test is not confined to Crown or other public bodies but also excludes any organisation (public or otherwise) performing that particular type of function. This does not affect questions of individual liability, and prosecutions for gross negligence manslaughter and other offences will remain possible against individuals performing these functions who are themselves culpable. The management of these functions will continue to be subject to other forms of accountability such as independent investigations, public inquiries and the accountability of Ministers through Parliament.

27. "Exclusively public functions" are defined in *section 3(4)*. The test covers both functions falling within the prerogative of the Crown (for example, where the Government provides services in a civil emergency) and *types* of activity that by their nature require a statutory or prerogative basis, in other words, that cannot be independently performed by private bodies. This looks at the nature of the activity involved. It therefore would not cover an activity simply because it was one that required a licence or took place on a statutory basis. Rather, the *nature* of the activity involved must be one that requires a statutory or prerogative basis, for example licensing drugs or conducting international diplomacy.

28. *Section 3(3)* provides that an organisation will not be liable in respect of any duty of care owed in connection with the carrying out of statutory inspections, unless the organisation owes the duty in its capacity as an employer or as an occupier of premises. This exemption would cover regulatory activities to ensure compliance with statutory standards: for example, inspection activities by the health and safety enforcing authorities. It is unlikely that these bodies would owe duties of care in respect of such activities or that these activities would be performed commercially; nor would the exercise of these functions amount to the supply of services. It is possible, though, that the carrying out of an inspection might involve the use of equipment, so as to bring section 2(1)(c)(iv) into play. This provision makes explicit that the performance of these functions will fall outside the scope of the offence.

Section 4: Military activities

29. Section 4 makes provision to exclude certain activities performed by the armed forces. A wide range of operational military activities will be exclusively public functions within the terms of section 3(2) and so exempt from the offence. However, that exemption does not relate to an organisation's duties as employer or occupier. Section 4 provides that certain military activities are exempt in respect of all categories of relevant duty of care. The exemption applies to the conduct, preparation and support of military operations as well as other hazardous and unpredictable circumstances, including peacekeeping operations and operations dealing with terrorism or serious public disorder. The law of negligence already recognises that the military authorities will rarely owe a duty of care in such circumstances. The fact that the Act will not apply in such circumstances is made explicit on the face of the Act. In addition, the exemption extends to training exercises that simulate these sorts of operations and to the activities of the special forces.

Section 5: Policing and law enforcement

30. Section 5 deals with policing and law enforcement activities performed by the police and other law enforcement bodies.

Subsection (1) provides an exemption that applies to the police and other law enforcement bodies in respect of all categories of duty of care referred to in section 2, i.e., including those duties of care owed by an organisation as an employer or the occupier of premises. But this wide exemption is available only in limited circumstances: specifically, operations dealing with terrorism, civil unrest or serious disorder in which an authority's officers or employees come under attack or the threat of attack; or where the authority in question is preparing for or supporting such operations; or where it is carrying on training with respect to such operations. This reflects the approach adopted in the existing law of negligence, which has already recognised that the policing of violent disorder where the police come under attack or the threat of attack will not give rise to liability on the part of an employer. The requirement in *section 5(2)* that the operations being carried on, or prepared for, or supported, amount to "policing or law enforcement activities" does not mean that only the police can benefit from this exemption: it is potentially available to bodies such as immigration authorities (*section 5(4)(d)*), and other bodies which in dealing with, say, civil disorder, are exercising functions similar to police functions. But it does mean that organisations that do not carry out policing and law enforcement activities are excluded from the scope of the exemption.

31.   *Subsection (3)* confers an exemption that applies to a wider range of policing and law enforcement activities, but not in respect of the duty of care owed as employer (or occupier). The exemption therefore operates to exclude circumstances where the pursuit of law enforcement activities has resulted in a fatality to a member of the public. Many of the activities to which this will be relevant will be ones that are not in any event covered by the offence either because no duty of care is owed or because they do not amount to the supply of services or the activities are exclusively public functions. However, this might not always be the case and some areas may give rise to question. Subsection (3) makes it clear that policing and law enforcement activities are not, in this respect, covered by the offence. This will include decisions about and responses to emergency calls, the manner in which particular police operations are conducted, the way in which law enforcement and other coercive powers are exercised, measures taken to protect witnesses and the arrest and detention of suspects. This exemption is not confined to police forces. It extends to other bodies operating similar functions and to other law enforcement activity. For example, it would cover the activities of Her Majesty's Revenue and Customs when conducting investigations and the activities of traffic officers. It also extends to the enforcement of immigration law, and so would cover circumstances where, for example, the immigration authorities are taking action to arrest, detain or deport an immigration offender.

32.   As with other matters not covered by the Act, this does not exempt individuals from investigation or prosecution for individual offences, as the Act does not have a bearing on the question of individual liability.

Section 6: Emergencies

33.   Section 6 clarifies that the offence does not apply to the emergency services when responding to emergencies. This does not exclude the responsibilities these authorities owe to provide a safe system of work for their employees or to secure the safety of their premises. Emergency circumstances are defined in terms of those that are life-threatening or which are causing, or threaten to cause, serious injury or illness or serious harm to the environment or buildings or other property. However, the exemption does not extend to medical treatment itself, or to decisions about this (other than decisions that establish the priority for treating patients). Matters relating to the organisation and management of medical services will therefore be within the ambit of the offence. The exemption also does not apply to duties that do not relate to *the way in which* a body responds to an emergency, for example, duties to maintain vehicles in a safe condition, which will similarly be capable of engaging the offence.

34.   The effect of exemption is therefore to exclude from the offence matters such as the timeliness of a response to an emergency, the level of response and the effectiveness of the way in which the emergency is tackled. Generally, public bodies such as fire authorities and the Coastguard do not owe duties of care in this respect and therefore would not be covered by the offence in any event. In some circumstances this may however be open to question. The new offence therefore provides a consistent approach to the application of the offence to emergency services, covering organisations in respect of their responsibilities to provide safe working conditions for employees and in respect of their premises, but excluding wider issues about the adequacy of their response to emergencies.

35.   The exemption extends to: fire and rescue authorities in the UK; other bodies responding to emergency circumstances by arrangement with a fire and rescue authority or on a non-commercial basis (such as organisations providing fire and rescue services at an airport under the terms of their aerodrome licence); NHS bodies and those providing ambulance services or the transport of organs or blood under contract to such a body; bodies such as the Coastguard and Royal National Lifeboat Institution; and the armed forces (who may be responding to emergency circumstances in respect of their own activities or providing assistance to civil authorities responding to an emergency). The exemption also applies to organisations carrying out rescue operations in emergency circumstances at sea, and to action taken to comply with safety directions (or taken in lieu of a direction) given by the Secretary of State under the Merchant Shipping Act 1995.

Section 7: Child-protection and probation functions

36.   Section 7 provides that the offence does not apply in relation to the exercise of specific functions to protect children from harm or in relation to the activities of probation services (or equivalent bodies in Scotland and Northern Ireland). The Act does not apply in relation to the exercise (or the failure to exercise) by local authorities of a number of specific statutory functions relating to decisions made to safeguard the welfare of children. The Act also does not apply in relation to the responsibilities of probation boards (or other equivalent public authorities) to supervise offenders or provide accommodation in approved premises. It is unlikely that such bodies would owe a duty of care should a person be killed in connection with such activities (for example, if a child was not identified as being at risk and taken into care and was subsequently fatally injured). This section makes it clear that such circumstances are not covered by the offence. Local authorities and probation services will however be covered by the offence in respect of responsibilities to their employees and in respect of the safety of the premises they occupy.

Section 8: Factors for jury

37.   Section 1(4)(b) sets out the test for assessing whether the breach of duty involved in the management failure was gross. The test asks whether the conduct that constitutes this failure falls far below what could reasonably have been expected. Whether this threshold has been met will be an issue for the jury to determine. The previous common law offence of gross negligence manslaughter asked whether the conduct was so negligent as to be criminal.

38.   To provide a clearer framework for assessing an organisation's culpability, section 8 sets out a number of matters for the jury to consider. In particular, these put the management of an activity into the context of the organisation's obligations under health and safety legislation, the extent to which the organisation was in breach of these and the risk to life that is involved. Section 8 also provides for the jury to consider the wider context in which these health and safety breaches occurred, including cultural issues within the organisation such as attitudes or accepted practices that tolerated breaches. When considering breaches of health and safety duties, juries may also consider guidance on how those obligations should be discharged. Guidance does not provide an authoritative statement of required standards and therefore the jury is not required to consider the extent to which this is not complied with. However, where breaches of relevant health and safety duties are established, guidance may assist a jury in considering how serious this was.

39.   These factors are not exhaustive and *section 8(4)* provides that the jury is also to take account of any other relevant matters.

Section 9: Remedial Orders

40.   In addition to the power under section 1 to impose an unlimited fine, section 9 gives the courts a power to order an organisation convicted of the new offence to take steps to remedy the management failure leading to death. It also enables the court to order the organisation to remedy any consequence of the management failure, if it appeared to the court to have been a cause of death. For example, where the management failure related to inadequate risk assessment and monitoring procedures, the consequence of which was inadequate safety precautions resulting in death, the court would be able to order the convicted organisation to improve both the management of risk and the resulting safety precautions. Remedial orders may also require an organisation to address deficiencies in health and safety management that lie behind the relevant breach of duty. For example, if the breach is indicative of the organisation and employees generally paying little attention to health and safety management, an order could require the organisation to review and communicate to staff its health and safety practices.

41.   Applications for remedial orders, setting out the proposed terms of the order, must be made by the prosecution, having consulted any relevant health and safety regulator. The convicted organisation will have an opportunity to make representations to the court about the order. The order must specify how long the organisation has to comply with the required steps and may require the organisation to supply evidence of compliance to any regulator consulted prior to the order being made. The compliance period can be extended on application. Failure to comply with a remedial order is an indictable-only offence for which the sanction will be an unlimited fine.

Section 10: Power to order conviction etc to be publicised

42.   Section 10 enables a court to order a convicted organisation to publicise, in a manner specified by the court, the fact of its conviction, specified particulars of the offence, the amount of any fine imposed and the terms of any remedial order that has been made. Prior to making an order the court is required to consult such regulatory bodies at it considers appropriate and to have regard to any representations made by the prosecution and defence. The order must specify the period within which the publicity must be made and may require the organisation to supply evidence of compliance to a regulator consulted prior to the order being set. Non-compliance with an order is an offence triable on indictment only and punishable with an unlimited fine.

Section 11: Application to Crown bodies

43.   The general presumption is that legislation does not apply to the Crown unless this is explicitly the case. *Section 11(1)* confirms the Act's application to the Crown and provides that the immunity that generally prohibits the prosecution of the Crown does not apply for the purposes of the new offence. Taken together, this provision and section 1 mean that Crown bodies that are either bodies corporate or are listed in Schedule 1 to the Act are subject to the new offence.

44.   The liability of the Crown in the law of negligence is governed by the Crown Proceedings Act 1947. This makes the Crown liable as an employer or occupier and also vicariously liable for the torts of its servants and agents. The new offence is, however, predicated on an organisation owing a personal duty of care to the victim. *Section 11(2)* bridges this difference by requiring Crown bodies to be treated as owing, for the purposes of the offence, the duties of care that they would owe if they were ordinarily constituted corporate bodies independent of the Crown.

45.   *Section 11(3)* and *(4)* addresses the fact that many of the activities and functions carried out by government departments and other Crown bodies are in law performed by the Crown rather than that body. For example, civil servants in government departments are employed by the Crown rather than the department for which they work. If provision were not made to deal with this, it might mean that the new offence did not work properly in its application to Crown bodies: conduct relevant to the offence might legally be attributable to the Crown rather than the body concerned and the employer's duty of care might technically be considered to be owed by the Crown rather than by the relevant department. These provisions ensure that the activities and functions of government departments and other Crown bodies can properly be attributed to the relevant body. *Section 11(5)* ensure that the relevant parts of these provisions apply to Northern Ireland departments, which are corporate bodies and therefore, although Crown bodies, do not need to be listed in Schedule 1 for the offence to apply.

Section 12: Application to armed forces

46.   Section 12 defines the term "armed forces" used in sections 4 and 6 of the Act so that it includes the Royal Navy, Army and Air Force. Section 12 also addresses the fact that technically members of the armed forces are not employed by the Ministry of Defence. Provision is required in the same way as described in paragraph 46 above to ensure that a duty of care as employer is owed to such personnel by the Ministry of Defence for the purposes of the offence.

Section 13: Application to police forces

47.   As police forces are not incorporated bodies, similar issues arise for the application of the offence to them as with Crown bodies. (This does not apply to police authorities, which are bodies corporate under the Police Act 1996 or the Police (Scotland) Act 1967 and to which the offence therefore applies separately and as for any other corporate body.) Section 13 therefore makes similar provision to section 12 and ensures that police officers are to be treated as the employees of the police force for which they work (and are therefore owed the employer's duty of care by the force); it also makes similar provision in relation to special constables and police cadets, police trainees in Northern Ireland and police officers seconded to the Serious Organised Crime Agency or National Policing Improvement Agency. It also ensures that police forces are treated as occupiers of premises and that other conduct is attributable to them as if they were distinctly constituted bodies.

Section 14: Application to partnerships

48.   Partnerships (other than limited liability partnerships, which are corporate bodies and covered by the new offence as such) are not corporations and so lack a distinct legal personality for the purpose of owing a duty of care in the law of negligence. Section 14 deals with this by providing for a partnership to be treated as though it owed the same duties of care as a corporate body for the purpose of this offence. Similarly, proceedings for the new offence are to be brought in the name of the partnership and any fine imposed on it is to be paid out of the funds of the partnership.

49.   These provisions are not required for partnerships that have a legal personality, as they do under (for example) Scots law. Nor are they required for trade unions or employers' associations in light of their quasi-corporate status.

Section 15: Procedure, evidence and sentencing

50.   Generally, provisions relating to criminal and court procedure, and sentencing, relate to the prosecution of individuals. Many of these will also be applicable to corporate bodies. Section 15 ensures that for the purposes of the new offence all such provisions apply, in the same way as they apply to corporations, to those Government departments or other bodies listed in Schedule 1, as well as to police forces and those unincorporated associations covered by the offence.

51.   Some separate provisions have been enacted to cater for the specific position of corporations. For example, section 33 of the Criminal Justice Act 1925 enables a corporation to plead through its representative as it cannot plead in person. Section 15 also enables any necessary modifications to be made to existing provisions by order. For example, a reference in the rules on criminal procedure to a director or the secretary of the corporation would need modification in order to apply to a department or police force. Such orders would be subject to the negative resolution procedure (that is, they are laid before Parliament and become law unless specifically annulled).

52.   Similar provision for Scotland can be achieved under the existing powers of the High Court to regulate procedure by Act of Adjournal.

Section 16: Transfer of functions

53.   This section makes provision for cases where functions have been transferred between (or out of) Government departments or other bodies listed in Schedule 1, incorporated Crown bodies or police forces. In summary, prosecutions will be commenced, or continued, against the body that *currently* has responsibility for the relevant function. But if the function is transferred out of the public sector entirely, proceedings will be against the body by which the function was last carried out. For machinery of Government changes, the effect of this is to place responsibility for defending proceedings with the organisation within which a function currently sits. But in order to retain the Crown's overall liability for proceedings if a function is transferred to a non-Crown body (for example, if a function were privatised), liability remains with the Crown body that previously performed the function.

54.   In some circumstances, a different approach might be warranted. For example, where a function transfers between Government departments but there is no corresponding transfer of personnel, it might be more appropriate for the department responsible at the time of the fatality to retain liability. Section 16 therefore includes provision for the Secretary of State to make an order specifying that liability rest with a different body. Such orders would be subject to the negative resolution procedure.

Section 17: DPP's consent required for proceedings

55.   The consent of the Director of Public Prosecutions (or DPP for Northern Ireland in the case of that jurisdiction) is needed for proceedings to be instituted. In Scotland all proceedings on indictment are instigated by the Lord Advocate. There is therefore no need for a consent mechanism.

Section 18: No individual liability

56.   Section 18 expressly excludes secondary liability for the new offence. Secondary liability is the principle under which a person may be prosecuted for an offence if they have assisted or encouraged its commission. In general, this means that a person can be convicted for an offence if they have aided, abetted, counselled

or procured it or, in Scotland, are guilty art and part. However, section 18 specifically excludes an individual being liable for the new offence on this basis. This does not though affect an individual's direct liability for offences such as gross negligence manslaughter, culpable homicide or health and safety offences, where the relevant elements of those offences are made out.

Section 19: Convictions under this Act and under health and safety legislation

57.   Section 19 clarifies that a conviction for corporate manslaughter would not preclude an organisation being convicted for a health and safety offence on the same facts if this were in the interests of justice. It would therefore also be possible to convict an individual on a secondary basis for such an offence under provisions such as section 37 of the Health and Safety at Work etc. Act 1974. This does not impose any new liabilities on individuals but ensures that existing liabilities are not reduced as an unintended consequence of the new offence.

Section 20: Abolition of liability of corporations for manslaughter at common law

58.   Section 20 abolishes the application of the common law offence of gross negligence manslaughter to corporate bodies and any application it has to those unincorporated associations to which the offence applies. Prosecutions for corporate manslaughter will in future fall under this legislation. This section does not affect the common law offence of culpable homicide in Scotland.

Section 21: Power to extend section 1 to other organisations

59.   Section 21 provides a power for the Secretary of State to apply the new offence to further categories of organisation, for example, to further types of unincorporated association. This is exercisable subject to the affirmative resolution procedure (that is, the relevant order will require approval in both Houses of Parliament before it comes into effect).

Section 22: Power to amend Schedule 1

60.   This section sets out the procedure for amending Schedule 1 (the list of Government departments and similar bodies to which the offence applies). Changes that are consequential on machinery of Government changes are to be made by the negative resolution procedure. This includes changes to the name of a particular department, as well as the addition of a department (if the reason for adding it is that it will have functions all of which were previously exercisable by another organisation to which the offence applies) or deletion of a department (again, if the reason is that all of its functions are being transferred to another organisation to which the offence applies, or if the department is being abolished). Other changes to Schedule 1 are subject to the affirmative resolution procedure. The effect is that changes which alter the range of activities or functions in relation to which the new offence applies will require a resolution by Parliament before they can come into effect, but otherwise the changes will take effect unless disapproved by Parliament.

Section 23: Power to extend section 2(2)

61.   Section 23 confers a power on the Secretary of State to extend the categories of person, listed in section 2(2), to whom a "relevant duty of care" is owed by reason of section 2(1)(d) - duties owed to a person because they are in custody or detention. The power enables further categories of person in custody or detention or in analogous circumstances to be added.

Section 24: Orders

62.   Orders under the Act are to be made through secondary legislation. Order-making powers (sections 15, 16, 21, 22 and 23) provide whether the order is to be made under the negative or affirmative resolution procedure. Section 24 defines these procedures. The commentary on these sections above describes the implication of this for each order-making power.

Section 25: Interpretation

63.   Section 25 defines various terms used in the Act including "corporation", "employee", "employer's association", "health and safety legislation", "partnership" and "trade union".

Section 26: Minor and consequential amendments

64.   Section 26 gives effect to Schedule 2 (see below).

Section 27: Commencement and saving

65.   *Section 27(1)* provides for the legislation to be brought into force by order - known as a commencement order - made by the Secretary of State. Other than in the case of section 2(1)(d), such an order will need to be laid before Parliament but is not subject to the affirmative or negative resolution procedure. An order commencing section 2(1)(d), that is commencing the offence in respect of duties owed a person because they are in custody or detention, is subject to the affirmative resolution procedure and will require approval in both Houses of Parliament before it takes effect.

66.   *Subsection (3)* makes it clear that the legislation is not retrospective. *Subsection (4)* makes provision for the common law offence of manslaughter by gross negligence to remain in place in respect to corporations for conduct and events that occur prior to commencement. Proceedings in respect of the common law offence (whether started before or after the new offence is brought into force) and arising out of the conduct and events occurring prior to commencement will not be affected by the Act.

Section 28: Extent and territorial application

67.   Section 28 deals with extent and territorial application. The Act extends to the whole of the United Kingdom. (Amendments to other legislation have the same extent as the provision they are amending: *section 28(2)*.)

68.   *Section 28(3)* and *(4)* set out the circumstances in which the courts will have jurisdiction for the new offence. Under section 10 of the Offences Against the Person Act 1861, courts in England and Wales have jurisdiction in a case of homicide if the injury causing death is inflicted in England and Wales, or in a place where the courts in England and Wales have jurisdiction (such as on a British ship), even if the death occurs elsewhere. The Act makes similar provision to this (but on a UK basis reflecting the application of the new offence across the UK), providing for jurisdiction if the harm causing death is sustained in the United Kingdom or other locations where criminal jurisdiction currently extends. Section 28(4) ensures that the offence will still apply if the harm resulting in death is sustained as a result of an incident involving a British ship (or aircraft or hovercraft), but the victim is not on board when he suffers that harm — for example, if a grave safety failing resulted in a ship being wrecked and the passengers being killed by drowning.

Section 29: Short title

69.   The short title of the Act is the Corporate Manslaughter and Corporate Homicide Act 2007. This reflects the fact that the offence will be known as corporate manslaughter in England and Wales and Northern Ireland, and corporate homicide in Scotland.

Schedule 1: List of Government departments etc

70.   The Schedule sets out the list of Government departments and other similar bodies to whom the offence applies. This does not cover Crown bodies that are incorporated (for example, such as the Health and Safety Commission and Executive) to which the offence applies by virtue of sections 1(2)(a) and 11(1) without further provision.

Schedule 2: Minor and consequential amendments

71.   Schedule 2 updates references to homicide offences in the Coroners Act 1988 to include the new offence and ensures that the term "person" in that Act is wide enough to include organisations capable of committing the new offence but which are not incorporated bodies. The Schedule also updates legislation in England and Wales and Northern Ireland that provides for a case to be retried in certain circumstances following acquittal and for appeals by the prosecution against certain terminating rulings. Previously, those provisions applied to specific, listed offences, including manslaughter (whether by individuals or a corporate body). These lists need amendment to reflect that future manslaughter proceedings against corporations will be for the new offence.

COMMENCEMENT

72.   The provisions of the Act will be brought into force by commencement order (see section 27(1)).

HANSARD REFERENCES

73.   The following table sets out the dates and Hansard references for each stage of the Act's passage through Parliament.

Stage	Date	Hansard reference
House of Commons (session 2005-06)		
Introduction	20 July 2006	Vol 449 Col 489
Second Reading	10 October 2006	Vol 450 Cols 191–267
Committee	19 October 2006; 24 October 2006; 26 October 2006; 31 October 2006	Hansard Standing Committee B
House of Commons (session 2006-07)		
Introduction	16 November 2006	Vol 453 Col 144
Second Reading	16 November 2006	Vol 453 Col 144
Report and Third Reading	4 December 2006	Vol 454 Cols 39–126
Commons Consideration of Lords Amendments	16 May 2007	Vol 460 Cols 662–707

Commons Consideration of Lords Reasons for Insisting on Certain Lords Amendments and for Disagreeing to the Commons Amendments in Lieu.	5 June 2007; 28 June 2007 and 11 July 2007	Vol 461 Cols 145–161; Vol 462 Cols 491–509 and Cols 1561–1578
Commons Consideration of Lords Insistence on Certain Lords Amendments, Disagreement to Commons Amendments in Lieu and Amendments in Lieu of those Commons Amendments.	18 July 2007	Vol 463 Cols 331–350
House of Lords (session 2006–07)		
Introduction	5 December 2006	Vol 687 Col 1061
Second Reading	19 December 2006	Vol 687 Cols 1896–1959
Grand Committee	11 January 2007; 15 January 2007; 17 January 2007 and 18 January 2007	Vol 688 Cols GC111–GC168, GC169–GC226, GC227–GC280 and GC281–GC308
Report	5 February 2007	Vol 689 Cols 497–544 and Cols 560–592
Third Reading	28 February 2007	Vol 689 Cols 1602–1609
Lords Consideration of Commons Disagreement to Certain Lords Amendments and Commons Amendments to the Bill in Lieu.	22 May 2007	Vol 692 Col 573–591
Lords Consideration of Commons Insistence on Disagreeing to Certain Lords Amendments and Commons Amendments in Lieu.	25 June 2007; 9 July 2007; 17 July 2007	Vol 693 Cols 447–464 and Cols 1262–1276; Vol 694 Cols 135–153
Lords Consideration of Commons Insistence on Disagreeing with Certain Lords Amendments, Disagreement with Lords Amendments in Lieu and further Commons Amendments in Lieu of Certain Lords Amendments	23 July 2007	Vol 694 Cols 553–564

Royal Assent—26 July 2007   House of Lords   Vol 694 Col 968
                                   House of Commons Vol 463 Col 1068

APPENDIX 2

Extract from Legislating the Criminal Code: Involuntary Manslaughter, *The Law Commission, Report No.237, 1996*

PART VIII
A NEW OFFENCE OF CORPORATE KILLING

INTRODUCTION

8.1   In Part VII we concluded that the use of the identification principle alone,[21] when applied to the individual offences that we recommend, would impose unacceptable limitations on the scope of corporate liability for involuntary homicide; that it would be wrong to adopt, solely for the purposes of the law of homicide, any wider principle of corporate liability such as vicarious liability or aggregation; and that it is therefore necessary to recommend the creation of a special offence, modelled on our proposed offence of killing by gross carelessness, but with such adaptation as is dictated by the peculiar characteristics of corporations. In this Part we consider what adaptation is required, and how the corporate offence should therefore be defined. We also consider a number of ancillary matters relating to the proposed offence.

8.2   For the offence of killing by gross carelessness, it must be proved

(1)   that the defendant's conduct caused the death,

(2)   that the risk of death or serious injury would have been obvious to a reasonable person in her position, and that she was capable of appreciating that risk, and

(3)   that her conduct fell far below what could reasonably be expected of her in the circumstances.[22]

FORESEEABILITY OF THE RISK

8.3   In our view, the second of these requirements cannot appropriately be applied to corporations, which, as Lord Hoffmann has recently emphasised,[23] are only metaphysical entities. To hypothesise a human being who *could* be in the same

---

[21]   We see no reason why the identification principle should not apply to our proposed offences in the comparatively unusual case where the necessary conditions for its application are satisfied—eg where the proprietor of a "one-man company" commits the offence of killing by gross carelessness in the course of running the company. See para 8.77 below.

[22]   The alternative, that she *intended* by her conduct to cause *some* injury, or was aware of, and unreasonably took, the risk that it might do so, may for present purposes be disregarded, since one of the reasons for adapting the offence for the purposes of corporate liability is the difficulty of attributing mens rea to a corporation: cf para 8.3 below.

[23]   *Meridian Global Funds Management Asia Ltd v The Securities Commission* [1995] 3 WLR 413, 419A; see para 6.4 [...].

position as the corporation is a logical impossibility,[24] and it would therefore be meaningless to enquire, as in the offence of killing by gross carelessness, whether the risk would have been "obvious" to such a person. Moreover, corporations have no "capacity", in the sense in which we use that term in this report in relation to an individual, so that it would be equally impossible to enquire whether the defendant corporation had the capacity to appreciate the risk. It is also, in our view, unnecessary. In judging the conduct of an individual defendant, the law must in fairness take account of such personal characteristics as may make it harder for her to appreciate risks that another person would appreciate; but the same considerations scarcely apply to a *corporate* defendant.

8.4   We have therefore concluded that the foreseeability of the risk, either to a hypothetical person in the defendant's position or to the defendant itself, should not be included in the definition of the corporate offence. This will not prevent juries from finding (in general terms) that the risk was, or should have been, obvious to any individual or group of individuals within the company who were or should have been responsible for taking safety measures, in deciding whether the company's conduct fell below the required standard. Nor would we wish to discourage the jury from approaching its task in that way. We are simply concerned, in formulating the new offence, to remove the *legal* requirement under the present law to identify individuals within the company whose conduct is to be attributed to the company itself.

SERIOUSNESS OF THE DEFENDANT'S CONDUCT

8.5   On the other hand we see no reason why the third requirement for the individual offence, that the defendant's conduct must have fallen *far* below what could reasonably be expected of her in the circumstances, should not apply equally to the corporate offence. This approach, as we have already explained,[25] is based on our view that the offence ought to be one of last resort, available only when all the other sanctions that already exist[26] seem inappropriate or inadequate, and that, therefore, the negligence in question must have been very serious.

8.6   We have therefore concluded, for the same reasons, that the new corporate offence should be committed only where the defendant's conduct fell far below what could reasonably be expected of it "in the circumstances". In our view, it would be neither practicable nor desirable to specify in legislation what those "circumstances" should or should not include: in every case it would be for the jury to decide whether the corporation's conduct fell within that description. In many cases this would involve the jury in balancing such matters as the likelihood and possible extent of the harm arising from the way in which the company conducted its operations against

---

[24]   This was pointed out by some respondents on consultation. The Chamber of Shipping, for example, suggested with some force that the question whether a *corporation* should have been aware of the risk is of "an entirely different kind" from the requirement, in the context of manslaughter by an individual, that the defendant should have been aware of the risk. It added that, since the jury would always be faced with the situation in which the risk had in fact eventuated, there was a danger of their being strongly tempted to conclude that the risk *must have been* one of which the company should have been aware.

[25]   Para 5.8 [...].

[26]   Eg the regulatory offences under ss 2 and 3 of the Health and Safety at Work etc Act 1974: see para 6.18 [...].

the social utility of its activities and the cost and practicability of taking steps to eliminate or reduce the risk of death or serious personal injury.[27]

8.7　The jury might also think it right to take account of the extent (if any) to which the defendant corporation's conduct diverged from practices generally regarded as acceptable within the trade or industry in question. This could not be conclusive, since the fact that a given practice is common does not *in itself* mean that the observance of that practice cannot fall far below what can reasonably be expected; but it might well be highly relevant.[28] The weight to be attached to it, if any, would be a matter for the jury.

CONDUCT OF THE DEFENDANT THAT CAUSES DEATH

8.8　Of the three requirements for the individual offence of killing by gross care-lessness, therefore, we envisage that the second (namely the obviousness of the risk, and the defendant's capacity to appreciate it) should be discarded for the purposes of the corporate offence, whereas the third (namely that the defendant's conduct in causing the death should have fallen far below what could reasonably be expected) should be retained. It remains to be determined what should be done about the first, namely that the defendant's conduct should have caused the death. Obviously that requirement must be retained in some form; equally obviously (in the light of the difficulties that we have explored in determining whether particular conduct can, under the present law, be regarded as the conduct of a company and not merely of its human agents), it must be adapted for the purposes of the corporate defendant. There are two aspects to this requirement: first, the defendant must have acted, or omitted to act, in a particular way; and second, the death must have resulted from that act or omission. In the case of an individual defendant it is rarely necessary to distinguish these two aspects: once the facts are known, there is no difficulty in distinguishing the defendant's conduct from someone else's. In the case of a *corporate* defendant, however, this distinction is problematic. Since we have rejected the option of attributing to the corporation *everything* done (or not done) by its agents, we must find a way of identifying that conduct which *can* properly be attributed to it. The question is: in what circumstances can it properly be said, not merely that the conduct of a corporation's *agents* has caused a death, but that the conduct of *the corporation itself* has done so?

Conduct of the defendant

8.9　In answering this question we have not had to start with an entirely clean slate. In the first place we have borne in mind the analogy of the identification principle laid down in *Tesco Supermarkets v Nattrass*,[29] which distinguishes between those agents of a company that qualify as its "controlling minds" and those that do not. As

---

[27]　Cf the recent decision (on employer's liability) of the Full Court of the High Court of Australia, *Miletic v Capital Territory Health Commission* 16 August 1995 (Australian Current Law, August 1995, 300). A housemaid cleaning a room in the nurses' quarters of a hospital fell and sustained injury while trying to move a bed on which the castors were jammed. The question was whether the employer was required to take preventive measures by way of routine maintenance against the likelihood of castors jamming and causing serious injury. Finding the employer liable, the court stated: (1) whether a reasonable person would take steps to avoid a foreseeable risk of injury to another was to be answered by balancing "the magnitude of the risk and the degree of the probability of its occurrence along with *the expense, difficulty and inconvenience of taking alleviating action and any other conflicting responsibilities which may exist*"; and (2) the duty to provide a safe place of work *required the balancing exercise* and could only result in the conclusion that a reasonable employer would carry out simple and inexpensive maintenance. (Emphasis added.)

[28]　Cf para 6.56 [...].

[29]　[1972] AC 153; [see also], paras 6.32–6.33, 6.35–6.39.

we have explained in Part VII above, we do not think that this principle is in itself sufficient for the imposition of corporate liability in every case of homicide where such liability would be justified; but the main reason for this is that the principle requires the prosecution to identify one or more "controlling minds" who are themselves guilty of a homicide offence. The distinction drawn in the *Tesco* case between things done in the management and organisation of the company on the one hand, and things done at a purely operational level on the other, seems to us to encapsulate the nature of the distinction that we need to draw. The difference between our approach and the identification principle is that we think the distinction should be drawn in terms of the *kind of conduct* that can incur liability, rather than the *status* of the person or persons responsible for it.

8.10   Secondly, we have drawn on the law governing an employer's common law obligation to take care for the safety of employees,[30] and one aspect of that obligation in particular—namely, the employer's duty to provide a safe system of work. This obligation is personal to the employer and is quite distinct from any *vicarious* liability that may arise in respect of injury caused to an employee by a fellow employee in the course of their employment. A breach of this obligation is not just negligence for which the employer is (vicariously) responsible: it is the employer's *own* negligence. The distinction thus corresponds to the distinction that we seek to draw, in the case of a corporate employer, between the conduct of the corporation and the conduct of its employees alone; and it is because of this analogy that we have taken this obligation as a starting-point in defining the kind of conduct that we propose as an element of the new corporate offence. In effect, we propose to use it as a model for the duty of *every* corporation to *all* those (not just employees) who may be affected by the corporation's activities.[31]

8.11   In a leading case in 1938 Lord Wright explained the general nature of the employer's obligation as

> a duty which rests on the employer and which is personal to the employer, to take reasonable care for the safety of his workmen, whether the employer be an individual, a firm, *or a company*, and

> whether or not the employer takes any share in the conduct of the operations.[32]

8.12   Lord Wright described the obligation as threefold: "the provision of a competent staff ... , adequate material, and a proper system and effective supervision". The doctrine of common employment was, however, still in existence in

---

[30]   The employer's obligation is not absolute: it can be performed by the exercise of due care and skill.

[31]   Other models may be thought equally useful: eg the liability of an occupier to her lawful visitors under the Occupiers' Liability Act 1957. The model of employer's liability does not *directly* resolve the problem of differentiating between negligence at managerial and operational levels, because even in tort it may be necessary to identify a controlling mind who is at fault before the company can be said to be in breach of its *personal* duty: see *Winfield and Jolowicz on Tort* (14th ed 1994) pp 716–717; *Street on Torts* (9th ed 1993) p 565. The analogy we seek to draw is not with tortious *corporate* liability in particular, but with the distinction between the *personal* liability of an employer (including an individual employer) and her *vicarious* liability for the negligence of her employees.

[32]   *Wilsons & Clyde Coal Co Ltd v English* [1938] AC 57, 84. (Emphasis added.)

1938.[33] Following the abolition of that doctrine ten years later, the obligation need no longer be put under three heads. It is a single duty, and "all other rules or formulas must be taken subject to this principle".[34] In practice, however, the duty may still be regarded as having several branches (which may overlap). The main branches are: (1) to provide a safe place of work, including a safe means of access; (2) to employ competent staff; (3) to provide and maintain adequate appliances; and (4) to provide a safe system of work.

8.13 An illustration of the first branch is provided by *Stafford v Antwerp Steamship Co Ltd*,[35] a case in which a stevedore was injured whilst loading a vessel. He fell into the hold through an open hatch after slipping on some ice as he tried to pass along the space between the case being loaded and the hatchway. The employers had caused or permitted cargo to be lowered and worked on in dangerous proximity to the edge, although climatic conditions rendered it likely that ice or frost would render the floor area slippery, and had failed to maintain any safety net in contemplation of such an incident.

8.14 The duty to employ competent staff is illustrated by *Hudson v Ridge Manufacturing Co Ltd*,[36] where an employee persistently engaged in "skylarking". For instance, he tripped up other employees, and took no notice of the foreman's reprimands. It was held that the employers were under a duty to remove the danger, by dismissal if necessary. In *Butler v Fife Coal Co Ltd*,[37] a man was killed by an outbreak of poisonous gas whilst working in the defendants' coal mine. The defendants were held liable not only under the Employers' Liability Act 1880 but also at common law, for breach of their duty to appoint and keep in charge persons competent to deal with the dangers arising in the mine. The under-manager and the fireman were negligent in that, despite being aware of a peculiarly smelling haze which had given some workmen headaches and nausea, they had failed to take steps to remedy the situation or evacuate the area.

8.15 The duty to provide and maintain adequate appliances is exemplified by *Taylor v Rover Co Ltd*,[38] where the plaintiff was injured by a piece of metal which had flown off a chisel he was using. The excessive hardness of the chisel had been identified a few weeks previously when a piece had broken off and injured another workman. This area of the law is now covered by section 1 of the Employer's Liability (Defective Equipment) Act 1969.[39]

---

[33] An employer, though vicariously liable to third parties for torts committed by her employees during the course of their employment, was not *vicariously* liable to one employee for harm sustained in consequence of a tort committed by another employee with whom she was in "common employment". The doctrine became subject to considerable judicial qualifications that restricted its scope. It was finally abolished by the Law Reform (Personal Injuries) Act 1948.

[34] *Cavanagh v Ulster Weaving Co Ltd* [1960] AC 145, 165, *per* Lord Keith.

[35] [1965] 2 Lloyd's Rep 104.

[36] [1957] 2 QB 348 (Streatfield J).

[37] [1912] AC 149.

[38] [1966] 1 WLR 1491.

[39] In *Coltman v Bibby Tankers Ltd* [1988] AC 276, where the design and construction of a vessel were defective so that she was unseaworthy and led to the death of the deceased during the course of his employment, it was held that the vessel was "equipment" within the meaning of the Act of 1969.

8.16   In the present context the duty to provide a safe system of work is of particular significance: it requires the company to plan its operations in advance with due regard to safety.[40] As the author of a leading textbook points out:

> [T]he state of the premises and plant, and the choice and supervision of personnel, fall especially within the employer's province. In adding as a further component the system of work, the law does no more than adopt and clarify a distinction accepted in everyday life. The employer is responsible for the general organisation of the factory, mine or other undertaking; in short, he decides the broad scheme under which the premises, plant and men are put to work. This organisation or "system" includes such matters as co-ordination of different departments and activities; the lay-out of plant and appliances for different tasks; the method of using particular machines or carrying out particular processes; the instruction of apprentices and inexperienced workers; and a residual heading, the general conditions of work, covering such things as fire precautions. An organisation of this kind is required—independently of safety—for the purpose of ensuring that the work is carried on smoothly and competently; and the principle of law is that in setting up and enforcing the system, due care and skill must be exercised for the safety of the workmen. Accordingly, the employer's personal liability for an unsafe system—independently of the negligence of fellow-servants—is not founded on an artificial concept, but is directly related to the facts of industrial organisation.[41]

8.17   The term "system of work" includes the organisation of the work, the way in which it is intended the work shall be carried out, the giving of adequate instructions (especially to inexperienced workers), the sequence of events, the taking of precautions for the safety of the workers at all stages, the number of such persons required to do the job, the part to be taken by the various persons employed and the time at which they should perform their respective tasks.[42] Further,

> it includes ... or may include according to circumstances, such matters as the physical layout of the job—the setting of the stage, so to speak—the sequence in which the work is to be carried out, the provision of proper cases of warnings and notices, and the issue of special instructions. A system may be adequate for the whole course of the job or it may have to be modified or improved to meet circumstances which may arise. Such modifications or improvements appear to me equally to fall under the head of system.[43]

8.18   By contrast with the employer's liability under sections 2 and 3 of the Health and Safety at Work etc Act 1974,[44] the company would not automatically be liable for the negligence (however gross) of an employee. We would adopt the distinction in the field of employer's liability that was explained in one case as follows:

> [B]roadly stated, the distinction is between the general and particular, between the practice and method adopted in carrying on the master's business of which the master is presumed to be aware and the insufficiency of which he can guard against, and isolated or day to day acts of the servant of which the master is not

---

[40]   "It is the duty of an employer to give such general safety instructions as a reasonably careful employer *who has considered the problem presented by the work* would give to his workmen": *General Cleaning Contractors Ltd v Christmas* [1953] AC 180, 189, *per* Lord Oaksey. (Emphasis added.)

[41]   J H Munkman, *Employer's Liability at Common Law* (11th ed 1990) pp 135–136.

[42]   *Charlesworth & Percy on Negligence* (8th ed 1990) p 819, para 10–59.

[43]   *Speed v Thomas Swift & Co Ltd* [1943] 1 KB 557, 563–564, *per* Lord Greene MR.

[44]   See the *British Steel* case, considered at paras 6.18–6.22 [...].

presumed to be aware and which he cannot guard against; in short, it is the distinction between what is permanent or continuous on the one hand and what is merely casual and emerges in the day's work on the other hand.[45]

8.19   Whether or not a system of work should be prescribed in any given case will depend on the circumstances: there is no doctrine of precedent to require cases to be followed where facts are similar.[46] The question is always: was "adequate provision made for the carrying out of the job in hand under the general system of work adopted by the employer or under some special system adapted to meet the particular circumstances of the case?"[47] We have adopted a similar approach for the corporate offence: under our recommendations, the crucial question would be whether the conduct in question amounted to a failure to ensure safety *in the management or organisation of the corporation's activities* (referred to as a "management failure" for short). This would be a question of fact for the jury to determine, and the discussion that follows must be viewed in the light of that overriding consideration.

8.20   Under our proposals, individuals within the company could be concurrently liable, in respect of an incident for which the company was liable, for the offence of killing by gross carelessness; and, whether or not they were so liable, their conduct might be relevant to the corporate offence as part of the circumstances surrounding that offence. For the purpose of the corporate offence and by contrast with the present law, however, there would be no need to identify the controlling officers of the company.[48] The question would be whether there had been a management failure, rather than, as at present, whether there was blameworthy conduct on the part of any individual or group of individuals which should be attributed to the company.[49]

8.21   To take a simple hypothetical example, if a lorry driver employed by a company causes death by dangerous driving in the course of the company's business, this act would not *of itself* involve a management failure so as to incur corporate liability;[50] nor would the company be *vicariously* liable for the driver's negligence. The company might be liable, however, if the incident occurred because the driver was overtired at the material time in consequence of a requirement to work excessively long hours, or because she consistently worked very long hours in her desire to earn overtime, and the company had no adequate system of monitoring to ensure that this did not happen.

8.22   Lord Keith's approach in the *Seaboard* case[51] gives a further illustration of the distinction between the "casual" negligence of a company's employee and the failure to provide a safe system of conducting the company's activities. He said:

---

[45]   *Wilsons and Clyde Coal Co Ltd v English* 1936 SC 883, 904, *per* Lord Aitchison (the Lord Justice-Clerk).

[46]   *Qualcast (Wolverhampton) Ltd v Haynes* [1959] AC 743.

[47]   *Winter v Cardiff Rural District Council* [1950] 1 All ER 819, 822, *per* Lord Porter.

[48]   The introduction of the new corporate offence would not affect the present law of corporate liability in its application to the other offences recommended in this report: see para 8.77 below. In cases such as *Kite and OLL Ltd* (the "Lyme Bay" case, para 6.48 [...]), therefore, the company could be convicted of killing by gross carelessness.

[49]   *Meridian Global Funds Management Asia Ltd v Securities Commission* [1995] 3 WLR 413 (PC) *per* Lord Hoffmann; see para 6.4 [...].

[50]   See Professor Sir John Smith's comment on *British Steel*: para 6.21, n 31 [...]. His suggestion accords with our approach in the context of the corporate offence.

[51]   *Seaboard Offshore Ltd v Secretary of State for Transport* [1994] 1 WLR 541, considered at paras 6.14–6.17 [...].

[I]t would be surprising if by the language used in section 31[52] Parliament intended that the owner of a ship should be criminally liable for any act or omission by any officer of the company or member of the crew which resulted in unsafe operation of the ship, ranging from a failure by the managing director to arrange repairs to a failure by the bosun or cabin steward to close portholes. . . . The steps to be taken are to be such as will secure that the ship is operated in a safe manner. That conveys to me the idea of *laying down a safe manner of operating the ship* by those involved in the actual operation of it and taking appropriate measures to bring it about that such safe manner is adhered to.[53]

8.23   We accept that there will be some cases in which the jury will have to draw a somewhat fine line between an employee's "casual" negligence and a management failure. Such cases abound in the field of employer's liability. We consider some of them in the following paragraphs, solely, we would emphasise, for the purpose of illustration. If a company was on trial for an offence that arose out of a death in circumstances similar to one of the cases cited, that case would be no authority on the question whether on the present occasion the company was guilty of a management failure, since this would be a question of fact to be decided by the jury.

8.24   The earliest case in which an employer's liability for failing to have a proper method of work can be traced is *Sword v Cameron*,[54] in which a workman employed in a stone quarry was injured by the explosion of a shot in the quarry in which he was working. The workmen were not given sufficient time to get clear before the explosion took place, and the Court of Session held that the employer was liable for failing to have a proper method of warning. Lord Cranworth later said of this decision:

> The injury was evidently the result of a defective system not adequately protecting the workmen at the time of the explosions. . . . The accident occurred, not from any neglect of the man who fired the shot, but because the system was one which did not enable the workmen at the crane to protect themselves by getting into a place of security.[55]

8.25   The inadequacy of the system in *Sword v Cameron* closely resembled that of the leading authority of *Wilsons and Clyde Coal Co v English*[56] in which the workmen were not given a sufficient period of time in which to reach a place of safety before certain operations in the mine began. The respondent in that case was injured whilst making his way to the pit bottom after having finished his morning shift. During the period in which the men finished their shift and left that part of the mine, the haulage plant was not stopped and the respondent was caught by a rake of hutches and crushed between it and the side of the road along which he was proceeding. The court held that it was a necessary part of a safe system of working that the haulage should be stopped on the main haulage roads during the period fixed for raising the day shift men up the pit. Lord Justice-Clerk Aitchison in the Court of Session[57] drew a distinction between

---

[52]   Of the Merchant Shipping Act 1988, which provides that it is the duty of the owner of certain ships to take all reasonable steps to secure that the ship is operated in a safe manner. See further para 6.17 [. . .]. (Footnote added.)

[53]   [1994] 1 WLR 541, 545E–G. (Emphasis added.)

[54]   (1839) 1 D 493.

[55]   *Bartonshill Coal Co v Reid* (1858) 3 Macq 290.

[56]   [1938] AC 57 (HL).

[57]   1936 SC 883.

the practice and method adopted in carrying on the master's business of which
the master is presumed to be aware and the insufficiency of which he can guard
against [and those] isolated or day-to-day acts of the servant of which the
master is not presumed to be aware and which he cannot guard against.[58]

8.26   In *Smith v Baker and Sons*,[59] the plaintiff was employed to drill holes in a rock
cutting near a crane worked by men in the same employment. The crane lifted stones
and at times swung them over the plaintiff's head without warning. A stone fell from
the crane, injuring the plaintiff. It was found by the jury that the machinery for lifting
the stone was not fit for the purpose for which it was applied, that the omission to
supply a special means of warning was a defect in the ways, works, machinery and
plant, and that the employers were guilty of negligence in not remedying the defect.
Lord Herschell described the duty as

the duty of taking reasonable care to provide proper appliances, and to
maintain them in a proper condition, and so to carry on his operations as not to
subject those employed by him to unnecessary risk.[60]

8.27   In *Speed v Swift (Thomas) & Co Ltd*[61] a ship was being loaded from a barge
alongside. In the course of the operation an empty hook, which was being brought
back to the ship's side, caught in a section of rail and caused it and a piece of timber
to fall, injuring the plaintiff. Although the system of work applied did not diverge
from the normal system of working expected, there were special circumstances with
regard to the particular ship in this instance which increased the danger and thus
necessitated extra precautions being taken. In view of this the employers had failed to
provide a safe and proper system of working adapted to the special circumstances.
Lord Greene MR emphasised that the duty should

be considered, not generally, but in relation to the particular circumstances of
each job.[62]

8.28   Lord Greene then proceeded to give a detailed, though not exhaustive,
account of what may amount to a "system".

I do not venture to suggest a definition of what is meant by system, but it
includes ... such matters as the physical lay-out of the job—the setting of the
stage, so to speak—the sequence in which the work is to be carried out, the
provision in proper cases of warnings and notices, and the issue of special
instructions.[63]

8.29   In *Colfar v Coggins and Griffiths (Liverpool) Ltd*[64] the facts were similar to
those in *Speed v Swift*,[65] yet the court reached a different conclusion. A dock labourer
was working in the hold of a ship stowing bags of salt, which were being lifted from a
barge by two derricks, which necessitated the fixing of one derrick arm by means of a
guy rope. The labourer was injured when several bags of salt fell from a swing into
the hold in which he was working, as a result of the derrick arm being inadequately
secured by the rope. It was held that the injury was attributable to the casual act of

[58]   *Ibid*, at p 904.
[59]   [1891] AC 325 (HL).
[60]   *Ibid*, at p 362.
[61]   [1943] 1 KB 557.
[62]   *Ibid*, at p 562.
[63]   *Ibid*, at p 563.
[64]   [1945] AC 197 (HL).
[65]   [1943] KB 557.

negligence committed by a fellow worker in reference to the guy rope, and was not a consequence of the system of work, it having not been found that placing so many bags of salt in one sling was negligent.

8.30   In *General Cleaning Contractors Ltd v Christmas*[66] a window cleaner was injured when the sash of the window he was working on came down on his hand, causing him to lose his balance and fall. It was held that although there was no evidence sufficient to establish negligence on the part of the employers in failing either to fix hooks for the safety belts into the building, or to cause the work to be done by means of ladders, they had failed to devise a safe system of work providing for an obvious danger, having neither given instructions to ensure that windows were tested before cleaning, nor provided any apparatus (such as wedges) to prevent them from closing. Leaving the taking of precautions to the initiative of their workers was a failure to discharge the duty to ensure a safe system of work.

8.31   In *Rees v Cambrian Wagon Works Ltd*[67] a heavy cog wheel was being removed by means of a plank and a sloping wedge in the course of dismantling a machine. The wheel overbalanced owing to the insufficiency of the wedge, and injured a workman. It was held that the operation required proper organisation and supervision, which the company had failed to provide.

8.32   In *Winter v Cardiff Rural District Council*,[68] by contrast, an employer was held not to have failed to provide a safe system where a heavy voltage regulator fell off a lorry on which it was being carried, carrying the plaintiff with it. The regulator had not been tied to the lorry, but the House of Lords held that the manner of the loading of the lorry was a routine matter within the discretion of the chargehand, and that the employers were not required to establish a proper system for such a routine task.

8.33   In *McDermid v Nash Dredging & Reclamation Co Ltd*,[69] the plaintiff, in the course of his employment as a deckhand with the defendant company, worked on board a tug owned by another company and under the control of a captain employed by it. The plaintiff's work included untying ropes that moored the tug to a dredger. The system used by the captain was that, when the plaintiff had untied the ropes and it was safe for the captain to move the tug, the plaintiff would give a signal. At the time in question the plaintiff was still in the course of untying one of the ropes when the captain, without waiting for the plaintiff's signal, put the engine of the tug hard astern. As a result, the plaintiff was injured. The House of Lords held that the defendant company was in breach of its duty to the plaintiff to provide a safe system of work for him: even if the captain's system of waiting for a signal was a safe system (which was doubtful), at the material time it "was ... not being operated and was therefore not being 'provided' at all".[70]

8.34   These cases are, we repeat, merely *illustrations* of how our proposed offence might work. Most of them concern the employer's duty to ensure a safe *system* of work; but there is no reason in principle why a "management failure" within the meaning of the proposed offence should not consist in a failure to provide safe premises or equipment, or competent staff. Nor do we suggest that the offence should be *defined* as hinging on whether the corporation's civil liability for the death would be personal or vicarious: in the context of criminal trials, such a test would be unworkable. The scope of an employer's personal duty of care is a model and no

---

[66]   [1953] AC 180.
[67]   (1946) 175 LT 220 (CA), approved by the House of Lords in *Winter*'s case (see n 48 below).
[68]   [1950] 1 All ER 819.
[69]   [1987] AC 906.
[70]   [1987] AC 906, 911F, *per* Lord Hailsham of St Marylebone.

more. But we believe that the distinction between "management failure" and operational negligence is an appropriate way of differentiating, in the context of involuntary homicide, between the conduct of a corporation and the conduct of its employees alone. Moreover, we would emphasise that a corporation would be liable only in extremely limited circumstances, namely where its conduct fell *far* below what could reasonably be expected of it in the circumstances. The offence would be confined to cases of very serious negligence.

8.35   **We therefore recommend**

(1)   **that there should be a special offence of corporate killing, broadly corresponding to the individual offence of killing by gross carelessness;**

(2)   **that (like the individual offence) the corporate offence should be committed only where the defendant's conduct in causing the death falls far below what could reasonably be expected;**

(3)   **that (unlike the individual offence) the corporate offence should *not* require that the risk be obvious, or that the defendant be capable of appreciating the risk; and**

(4)   **that, for the purposes of the corporate offence, a death should be regarded as having been caused by the conduct of a corporation if it is caused by a failure, in the way in which the corporation's activities are managed or organised, to ensure the health and safety of persons employed in or affected by those activities. (Recommendation 11)**

CAUSATION OF DEATH

8.36   Our proposed concept of "management failure" is an attempt to define what, for the purposes of a corporate counterpart to the individual offence of killing by gross carelessness, can fairly be regarded as unacceptably dangerous conduct *by a corporation*. But it must of course be proved, as in the individual offence, that the defendant's conduct (which, in the present context, means the management failure) *caused* the death. To a large extent this will involve the application of the ordinary principles of causation, as in any other homicide offence. If, for example, the jury are not satisfied beyond reasonable doubt that the death would not have occurred had it not been for the management failure, the offence will not be proved. Even if the death would not otherwise have occurred, it will be open to the jury to conclude that the "chain of causation" was broken by some unforeseeable act or event, and that the management failure was not itself a cause of the death but merely part of the events leading up to it. If, for example, the management failure consisted of a failure to ensure that some potentially dangerous operation was properly supervised, a jury would be unlikely to conclude that this failure *caused* the death if the immediate cause was a *deliberate* act by an employee rather than a merely careless one—even if that act would probably not have occurred had a supervisor been present.

8.37   However, we think that the scope for any defence of a "break in the chain of causation" should be very limited. In many, perhaps most, cases it will be the operational negligence of one or more of the company's employees that is most closely connected in point of time with the death. For example, the immediate cause of the death might be the failure of an employee, through lack of attention, to give a signal which she was employed to give. Indeed, depending on the circumstances, the employee in question may personally be guilty of our proposed offence of killing by gross carelessness. It does not, in our view, follow that the employee's conduct should in itself absolve the *corporation* from liability, because the management failure may have consisted in a failure to take precautions against the very kind of error that in fact occurred. If a company chooses to organise its operations as if all its employees were paragons of efficiency and prudence, and they are not, the company is at fault; if an employee then displays human fallibility, and death results, the company cannot be permitted to deny responsibility for the death on the ground that the employee was to blame. The company's fault lies in its failure to anticipate the foreseeable negligence of its employee, and any consequence of such negligence should therefore be treated as a consequence of the company's fault.

8.38   It is not clear how far the ordinary law of causation takes account of this reasoning.[71] As Professor Ashworth has explained:

> [T]he principle of individual autonomy presumes that, where an individual who is neither mentally disordered nor an infant has made a sufficient causal contribution to an occurrence, it is inappropriate to trace the causation any further. This is taken to justify not only picking out D's conduct from other possible causes and regarding that conduct as operating on a "stage already set",[72] but also declining to look behind D's conduct for other persons who might be said to have contributed to D acting as he or she did.[73]

8.39   In our view, therefore, there is a danger that, without more, the application of the ordinary rules of causation would in many cases result in a management failure being treated as a "stage already set", and hence not linked in law to the death.[74] In our view the legislation should include an express provision to the effect that in this kind of situation the management failure may be *a* cause of the death, even if the *immediate* cause is the act or omission of an individual.[75] Whether in all the circumstances the management failure *is* a cause of the death, in spite of the intervening

---

[71] Cf Celia Wells, *Corporations and Criminal Responsibility* (1993) p 43:
I have called legal causation a non-issue to emphasize the futility of the traditional search for separate principles by which to impute cause beyond the factual "but for" level. This of course does not mean that any "but for" contribution must lead to legal attribution, but that taking any steps beyond "but for" means *entering a complex terrain of responsibility attribution which is connected to issues beyond those of cause.* Whether a result was a *sine qua non* of the defendant's act is a necessary but not sufficient condition for imputing cause. (Emphasis added to second sentence.)

[72] See H L A Hart and T Honoré, *Causation in the Law* (2nd ed 1985), ch 1 and *passim*, and the derivative discussions by S Kadish, *Blame and Punishment* (1987), ch 8, and H Beynon, "Causation, Omissions and Complicity" [1987] Crim LR 539; cf also Williams, *Textbook of Criminal Law*, ch 14. (Footnote in original.)

[73] *Principles of Criminal Law* (2nd ed 1995) p 123. Cf J H Munkman, *Employer's Liability at Common Law* (11th ed 1990) p 62:
Reduced to its simplest terms, the question in each case is this: What factors actually *brought about* the accident?—as distinct from factors which merely *led up* to it. (Emphasis in original.)

[74] Cf Draft Criminal Code, Law Com No 177 (1989) vol 1, cl 17. The clause was intended to be a statement of existing common law principles (*ibid*, vol 2, para 7.14). It provides, so far as material:
(1) Subject to [subsection] (2) ..., a person causes a result which is an element of an offence when—
   (a) he does an act which makes a more than negligible contribution to its occurrence; or
   (b) he omits to do an act which might prevent its occurrence and which he is under a duty to do according to the law relating to the offence.
(2) A person does not cause a result where, after he does such an act or makes such an omission, an act or event occurs—
   (a) which is the *immediate and sufficient* cause of the result;
   (b) which he did not foresee; and
   (c) which could not in the circumstances reasonably have been foreseen. (Emphasis added.)
As to paras (b) and (c) of subs (2), foreseeability is inapplicable to the corporate offence: see paras 8.3–8.4 above.

[75] See cl 4(2)(b) of the draft Bill at Appendix A [...].

act or omission of an individual, will be a matter for the common sense of the jury. **We recommend that, for the purposes of the corporate offence, it should be possible for a management failure on the part of a corporation to be a cause of a person's death even if the immediate cause is the act or omission of an individual. (Recommendation 12)**

INDEPENDENT CONTRACTORS

The issue

8.40   A corporation may employ an independent contractor to carry out work in a variety of situations. One who engages an independent contractor is not normally liable to others for the negligence of that contractor; and an employer's duty of care in tort does not render her liable to her employees for injury sustained through the negligence of her contractor, save in exceptional circumstances.[76] The question whether an employer is criminally liable for such injury has recently arisen in the context of the offence under section 3(1) of the Health and Safety at Work etc Act 1974.[77] We first consider this recent development and then explain how we envisage that the matter would be approached under the corporate offence that we recommend.

The offence under section 3(1) of the Health and Safety at Work etc Act 1974

8.41   Section 3(1) of the 1974 Act refers to the duty of every employer to "conduct his undertaking" in such a way as to avoid exposure to risk.[78] There are two possible approaches to the construction of this phrase. On the narrower construction,[79] the employer's duty is coterminous with the employer's common law duty of care to those not in her employment, and it does not therefore (save in exceptional cases)[80] involve liability for the acts of independent contractors. On the wider construction, the expression is not confined to imposing criminal liability on an employer for a breach of her duty of care and extends to work necessary for the conduct of the employer's enterprise. The Court of Appeal recently adopted the wider construction in *Associated Octel Co Ltd.*[81] The court made it clear that the offence was concerned

---

[76]   There are several exceptions. They include the case in which the employer fails to coordinate the activities of subcontractors (*McArdle v Andmac Roofing Co* [1967] 1 WLR 356). Another exception arises where the employer exercises control over the contractor's operations, in the sense that she can tell the contractor's employees what to do and what safety precautions to adopt, or where she exercises joint or partial control over them in that respect (see, eg, *Associated Octel Co Ltd* [1994] 4 All ER 1051, 1057b–c).

[77]   See paras 6.18–6.22 [...].

[78]   See para 6.18 [...].

[79]   Applied in, eg, *RMC Roadstone Products Ltd v Jester* [1994] IRLR 330 (DC). The defendant company (R) manufactured road-making materials. They engaged X and Y, a firm of general repairers, to replace asbestos sheeting on the side of a transfer tower on their premises. Although the original intention was to use new sheets, X and Y obtained permission from the owners of adjacent premises to remove old asbestos sheets from the roof of a disused loading bay. R's loading manager warned the men of the dangers of working on an asbestos roof but (apart from lending them a front-loading shovel which they used to gain access to the roof, and to lower and transport the sheeting) left them to get on with the job. While working on the roof, X fell through a skylight and was fatally injured. It was held that the events leading to the death were not within the ambit of R's undertaking: X and Y had been left to do the work as they pleased. Smith J (with whose judgment Ralph Gibson LJ agreed) accepted, however, that where the employer had actual control over an activity and either exercised that control or was under a duty to do so, the activity would fall within the employer's conduct of her undertaking.

[80]   See para 8.40, n 56 above.

[81]   [1994] 4 All ER 1051.

with a wider spectrum of activities than those under the company's control.[82] All that the prosecution had to show, the court held, was that the activity in question was part of the conduct of the employer's undertaking. It was then for the employer to show, if she could, that it was not "reasonably practicable" to prevent the accident.[83]

8.42   Stuart-Smith LJ, giving the judgment of the court, said:

> The word "undertaking" means "enterprise" or "business". The cleaning, repair and maintenance of plant, machinery and buildings necessary for carrying on business is part of the conduct of the undertaking, whether it is done by the employer's own employees or by independent contractors. If there is a risk of injury ..., and, a fortiori, if there is actual injury as a result of the conduct of that operation, there is prima facie liability, subject to the defence of reasonable practicability.[84]

8.43   Stuart-Smith LJ emphasised that the question of control might, however, be "very relevant" in relation to the question of reasonable practicability, which was a matter of fact and degree in every case. On the one hand, where specialist contractors were instructed, it might not be reasonably practicable for the employer to do otherwise than rely on those contractors to see that the work was carried out safely. There were, on the other hand, cases where it was reasonably practicable for her to give instructions on how the work was to be done and what safety measures were to be taken. It would depend on

> a number of factors so far as concerns operations carried out by independent contractors; what is reasonably practicable for a large organisation employing safety officers or engineers contracting for the services of a small contractor on routine operations may differ markedly from what is reasonably practicable for a small shopkeeper employing a local builder on activities on which he has no expertise. The nature and gravity of the risk, the competence and experience of the workmen, the nature of the precautions to be taken are all relevant considerations.[85]

Independent contractors and the proposed corporate offence

8.44   We believe that there is no need to make specific provision in the present context in relation to the employment of a contractor by the company. In every case it will be for the jury to determine (1) whether a death of which the immediate cause was the conduct of a contractor employed by the company was attributable, at least in part, to a management failure on the part of the company, and (2) if so, whether that failure amounted to conduct falling far below what could reasonably be expected of the company in the circumstances.[86] It may well be that in particular

---

[82]   One commentator, G Holgate, "Employer's Liability: Reconstructing Section 3(1) of the Health and Safety at Work etc Act 1974" (1995) 159 JPN 385, 386, suggests that
Associated Octel is a most important decision which can only enhance workplace health and safety. ... In order to avoid liability, the prudent employer/principal will henceforth be well advised to adopt a "hands on" approach to the activities of contractors engaged by them, stipulating the necessary safety precautions and procedures and ensuring that they are complied with.

[83]   The question of control may be relevant to *that* issue; see para 8.43 below.

[84]   *Associated Octel Co Ltd* [1994] 4 All ER 1051, at pp 1062j–1063a. Under s 40 of the 1974 Act the burden of establishing the defence is placed on the defendant employer.

[85]   *Associated Octel Co Ltd* [1994] 4 All ER 1051, at p 1063f–h.

[86]   By contrast with the regulatory offence under s 3(1) of the 1974 Act (see para 8.41 above), the burden of proof will rest on the prosecution in respect of every element of the offence.

cases the jury will take into account all or some of the matters referred to by Stuart-Smith LJ in the passage cited in paragraph 8.43 above.

AN ILLUSTRATION

8.45   We will now show how we envisage the new offence would operate by reference to the 1987 Zeebrugge ferry disaster, which involved the "roll-on roll-off" passenger and freight ferry, *Herald of Free Enterprise*.[87] The ferry set sail from Zeebrugge inner harbour and capsized four minutes after crossing the outer mole, with the loss of 150 passengers and 38 crew members. The immediate cause of the capsize was that the ferry had set sail with her inner and outer bow doors open. The responsibility for shutting the doors lay with the assistant bosun, who had fallen asleep in his cabin, thereby missing the "Harbour Stations" call and failing to shut the doors. The Chief Officer was under a duty as loading officer of the G deck to ensure that the bow doors were closed, but he interpreted this as a duty to ensure that the assistant bosun was at the controls. Subsequently, the report of the inquiry by Mr Justice Sheen into the disaster ("the Sheen Report") said of the Chief Officer's failure to ensure that the doors were closed that, of all the many faults which combined to lead directly or indirectly to this tragic disaster, his was the most immediate.[88] The Chief Officer could in theory have remained on the G deck until the doors were closed before going to his harbour station on the bridge. However, although this would have taken less than three minutes, loading officers always felt under such pressure to leave the berth immediately that this was not done.[89]

8.46   The Master of the ferry on the day in question was responsible for the safety of the ship and those on board. The inquiry therefore found that in setting out to sea with the doors open he was responsible for the loss of the ship. The Master, however, had followed the system approved by the Senior Master, and no reference was made in the company's "Ship's Standing Orders" to the closing of the doors. Moreover, this was not the first occasion on which the company's ships had gone to sea with doors open, and the management had not acted upon reports of the earlier incidents.

8.47   The Senior Master's functions included the function of acting as co-ordinator between all the Masters who commanded the *Herald* and their officers, in order to achieve uniformity in the practices adopted on board by the different crews. He failed to enforce such orders as had been issued, and also failed to issue orders relating to the closing of the bow doors on G deck. The Sheen Report found that he "should have introduced a fail-safe system".

8.48   The criticism in the Sheen Report did not stop with those on board the ship:

> [F]ull investigation into the circumstances of the disaster leads inexorably to the conclusion that the underlying or cardinal faults lay higher up in the Company [than the Master, the Chief Officer, the assistant bosun and the Senior Master]. The Board of Directors did not appreciate their responsibility for the safe management of their ships. They did not apply their minds to the question: What orders should be given for the safety of our ships? The directors did not have any proper comprehension of what their duties were. There appears to have been a lack of thought about the way in which the *Herald* ought to have been organised for the Dover/Zeebrugge run. All concerned in management,

---

[87]   See paras 6.49—6.56 [...].
[88]   MV *Herald of Free Enterprise*: Report of the Court (No 8074), Department of Transport (1987), para 10.9.
[89]   The Sheen Report pointed out (at para 11.2) that the guide issued by the company created a conflict in the loading officer's duties.

from the members of the Board of Directors down to the junior super-intendents, were guilty of fault in that all must be regarded as sharing responsibility for the failure of management. From top to bottom the body corporate was infected with the disease of sloppiness. . . . The failure on the part of the shore management to give proper and clear directions was a contributory cause of the disaster.[90]

8.49   As we explained [. . .],[91] the prosecution against P & O European Ferries (Dover) Ltd ultimately failed. The judge directed the jury that, as a matter of law, there was no evidence upon which they could properly convict six of the eight defendants, including the company, of manslaughter.[92] The principal ground for this decision in relation to the case against the company, was that, in order to convict it of manslaughter, one of the individual defendants who could be "identified" with the company would have himself to be guilty of manslaughter. Since there was insufficient evidence on which to convict any of those individual defendants, the case against the company had to fail.[93]

8.50   If circumstances such as these were to occur again, we think it would probably be open to a jury to conclude that, even if the immediate cause of the deaths was the conduct of the assistant bosun, the Chief Officer or both, another of the causes was the failure of the company to devise a safe system for the operation of its ferries; and that that failure fell far below what could reasonably have been expected. In these circumstances the company could be convicted of our proposed new offence.

POTENTIAL DEFENDANTS

Corporations

8.51   We consider that the new offence should extend to all corporations, irrespective of the legal means by which they are incorporated. This would include not only those incorporated under a general public Act (such as the Companies Act 1985) but also those incorporated at common law (such as the Corporation of London), by royal charter (such as the BBC, and most universities), by private or local Act (such as certain public utility companies) or special public Act (including a number of organisations in the public sector). Most of these corporations have no shareholders and are not run with a view to profit, but we do not regard this as a reason for exempting them from the rules applicable to other corporations.

8.52   We also think that the offence should extend to corporations incorporated abroad. If a death results from the mismanagement of a company, we see no reason why the company's liability should be affected by the place where it happens to have been incorporated, any more than the liability of an individual (for things done in England and Wales) is affected by her nationality. We do not propose, in general, that the offence should be committed where the fatal injury occurs outside England and Wales; but this is a question of the offence's territorial extent. It does not follow that foreign corporations should be immune from prosecution in respect of fatal accidents that do occur in England and Wales.

8.53   However, we propose that corporations sole should be excluded. A corporation sole is a corporation constituted in a single person in right of some office or

---

[90]   *Ibid*, para 14.1.
[91]   Paras 6.49–6.56 [. . .]; and see Consultation Paper No 135, para 4.31.
[92]   *Stanley and others* 19 October 1990 (CCC No 900160), unreported.
[93]   In coming to this conclusion Turner J ruled against the adoption into English criminal law of the "principle of aggregation": *Stanley and others* 19 October 1990 (CCC) unreported transcript pp 8E–9C. See para 6.50 [. . .].

function, which grants that person a special legal capacity to act in certain ways: examples are government ministers and archbishops.[94] The corporation sole is in reality a legal device for differentiating between an office-holder's personal capacity and her capacity *qua* holder of that office for the time being. It is expressly excluded from the definition of a corporation in section 740 of the Companies Act 1985, and we exclude it from our proposed corporate offence as well. **We recommend that the offence of corporate killing should be capable of commission by any corporation, however and wherever incorporated, other than a corporation sole. (Recommendation 13)**

Unincorporated bodies

8.54   We have considered whether the proposed new offence should apply to partnerships, trusts (such as hospital trusts) and other unincorporated bodies. Many such organisations are for practical purposes indistinguishable from corporations, and it is arguable that their liability for fatal accidents should be the same. However, we have concluded that it would be inappropriate for us to recommend such an extension of the offence at the present time. Under the existing law the individuals who comprise an unincorporated body may be criminally liable for manslaughter, as for any other offence; and, by contrast with the law relating to corporations, the question of attributing the conduct of individuals to the body itself does not arise. In this respect the law will be unaffected by the replacement of manslaughter with the offences in the draft Bill of reckless killing and killing by gross carelessness.

8.55   It would clearly be wrong to extend the offence to *all* unincorporated bodies, because there are many such bodies (for example, a partnership of two individuals, employing no-one) that would be unfairly disadvantaged by being charged with the corporate offence (which does not require foreseeability)[95] rather than that of killing by gross carelessness (which does). Any extension of the offence beyond incorporated bodies would therefore raise intractable problems as to the *kinds* of unincorporated body that ought and ought not to be included. But there has been no consultation on any proposal to this effect, either in the consultation paper or in any other form. We think it would be wise to await experience of the operation of our proposed corporate offence, in the context of the kind of organisation for which it is primarily designed—namely the commercial corporation—before considering whether to extend it further. **We recommend that the offence of corporate killing should not be capable of commission by an unincorporated body. (Recommendation 14)**

Secondary parties

8.56   A provision imposing liability on the officers of a company is commonly included in legislation creating an offence likely to be committed by a corporation. The Health and Safety at Work etc Act 1974, for example, provides:

> Where an offence under any of the relevant statutory provisions committed by a body corporate is proved to have been committed with the consent or connivance of, or to have been attributable to any neglect on the part of, any

---

[94]   It has no connection with a company having a single member—something which, in the UK, can now exist by virtue of the Companies (Single Member Private Limited Companies) Regs 1992, SI 1992 No 1699, made in pursuance of EC Council Directive No 89/667/EEC.

[95]   See para 8.4 above.

director, manager,[96] secretary or other similar officer of the body corporate or a person who was purporting to act in any such capacity, he as well as the body corporate shall be guilty of that offence ... .[97]

8.57   Even in the absence of such a provision, an individual may be liable under the general law[98] as a secondary party, for aiding, abetting, counselling or procuring an offence committed by a corporation, just as she may be party to one committed by another individual.

8.58   We intend that no individual should be liable to prosecution for the corporate offence, even as a secondary party. Our aim is, first, that the new offences of reckless killing and killing by gross carelessness should replace the law of involuntary manslaughter for individuals; and second, that the offence of killing by gross carelessness should be adapted so as to fit the special case of a corporation whose management or organisation of its activities is one of the causes of a death. The indirect extension of an *individual's* liability, by means of the new corporate offence, would be entirely contrary to our purpose. There will no doubt be many cases in which the conduct of one or more of the company's employees will amount to the commission of one of the two "individual" offences; but where that conduct does not fulfil the requirements of liability for one of those two offences, we would not wish an individual employee to be caught by the corporate offence. We doubt whether, in practice, it would be possible for an individual employee to be a secondary party to the corporate offence without committing the offence of reckless killing or that of killing by gross carelessness; but we take the view that it is desirable, by means of express legislative provision, to obviate the need for prosecutors and courts even to consider the question of secondary liability for the corporate offence. **We recommend that the offence of corporate killing should not be capable of commission by an individual, even as a secondary party. (Recommendation 15)**

TERRITORIAL JURISDICTION

8.59   The general rule is that nothing done outside England and Wales is an offence under English criminal law.[99] In the case of homicide by an individual, however, the English courts have jurisdiction in the following cases:

(1)   Section 9 of the Offences Against the Person Act 1861 confers jurisdiction over a homicide committed by a British subject on land outside the United Kingdom.

(2)   Section 2 of the Territorial Waters Jurisdiction Act 1878 confers jurisdiction over offences committed on ships (including foreign ships) in British territorial waters.[100]

---

[96]   The word "manager" in this type of provision refers to someone of real authority, with the power and the responsibility to decide corporate policy: she must perform a governing role in the company's affairs rather than one of day-to-day management: see, eg, *Boal* [1992] 1 QB 591. (Footnote added.)

[97]   Section 37(1). The definition of "relevant statutory provisions" in s 53(1) of the Act includes ss 2 and 3 of the Act (considered at paras 6.18—6.22 [...]).

[98]   Accessories and Abettors Act 1861, s 8 (as amended by the Criminal Law Act 1977, s 65(4), Sch 12). The section, which placed the common law on a statutory footing, provides:

Whosoever shall aid, abet, counsel or procure the commission of any indictable offence whether the same be an offence at common law or by virtue of any act passed or to be passed, shall be liable to be tried, indicted, and punished as a principal offender.

Section 44 of the Magistrates' Courts Act 1980 contains similar provision for summary offences. We examined the principles applicable in Assisting and Encouraging Crime (1993) Consultation Paper No 131.

[99]   See G Williams, "Venue and the Ambit of Criminal Law" (1965) 81 LQR 276, 395, 518.

[100]   But not foreign aircraft in flight over territorial waters.

(3) Section 686(1) of the Merchant Shipping Act 1894[101] confers jurisdiction over offences committed on British ships, even in foreign waters.

(4) Section 92 of the Civil Aviation Act 1982 confers jurisdiction over offences committed on British-controlled aircraft while in flight elsewhere than in or over the United Kingdom.

(5) The Criminal Jurisdiction (Offshore Activities) Order 1987,[102] made under section 22 of the Oil and Gas (Enterprise) Act 1982, confers jurisdiction over offences committed on, under or above an "installation"[103] in British territorial waters or certain parts of the continental shelf, or within 500 metres of such an installation.

8.60   Where a particular offence consists in the bringing about of a particular result, the place where the offence is committed is normally the place where that result occurs. In the case of homicide, however, section 10 of the Offences Against the Person Act 1861 confers jurisdiction

(1) where the *injury* is inflicted in England and Wales, even if the death occurs elsewhere; or

(2) where the *death* occurs in England and Wales, even if the injury is inflicted elsewhere;

but it has been held that the latter rule applies only if the injury is inflicted within the jurisdiction of the English courts, for example on a British ship.[104]

8.61   We see no reason why the rules relating to the territorial extent of our proposed offences of *individual* homicide should be different from those that now apply to manslaughter, and we make no recommendation on this issue: the existing rules would thus apply to our proposed individual offences. We also think that, for the most part, the same principles should apply, as far as possible, to the corporate offence. Thus, subject to the other requirements of the offence, it would be committed if the injury that results in the death is sustained in such a place that the English courts would have had jurisdiction over the offence if it had been committed by an individual—that is, in England and Wales, on any vessel in territorial waters or a British vessel elsewhere,[105] on a British-controlled aircraft in flight outside the United Kingdom, or in any place to which an Order in Council under section 22 of the Oil and Gas (Enterprise) Act 1982 applies.

8.62   However, we do not propose that the corporate offence should be extended by a provision corresponding to section 9 of the Offences Against the Person Act, which confers jurisdiction over homicides committed by British subjects abroad. Such a provision would presumably involve extending the offence to deaths resulting from management failures by *British* companies, even where the injury is sustained abroad. We see no pressing need for such a provision, since there might well be liability under foreign law in such a case; we think it likely (though we have not investigated the matter) that the considerations affecting the liability of British companies are different from those affecting the liability of British citizens; and there has been no consultation on the matter. **We recommend that there should be liability for the corporate offence only if the injury that results in the death is sustained in such a place that the English courts would have had jurisdiction over the offence had it been committed by an individual other than a British subject. (Recommendation 16)**

---

[101]   As amended by the Merchant Shipping Act 1993, s 8(3).
[102]   SI 1987 No 2198.
[103]   Ie "any floating structure or device maintained on a station by whatever means".
[104]   *Lewis* (1857) Dears & B 182, 169 ER 968.
[105]   Thus it would extend to the circumstances of the Zeebrugge ferry disaster.

CONSENT TO PROSECUTION

8.63   We are very conscious of the strength of feeling understandably engendered by fatal accidents, and of how much pressure there can be for a prosecution. At present it is initially for the Crown Prosecution Service ("CPS") to decide whether there is sufficient evidence to offer a realistic prospect of a conviction, and (if so) whether the public interest requires a prosecution;[106] but if the CPS decides not to prosecute, on either ground, a private individual (such as a relative of the deceased) may either seek judicial review of the decision[107] or bring a private prosecution.[108] The CPS has power to take over a private prosecution and discontinue it,[109] but will not necessarily think it appropriate to do so merely because it decided not to institute proceedings itself. A decision to discontinue may be open to judicial review.[110] Private prosecutions are also controlled to some extent by the magistrates' court. In the first place the court can decline to issue a summons if the proceedings appear to be vexatious; but such a refusal can itself be challenged by judicial review. Secondly, the defendant can at present ask for an "old-style" committal hearing and submit that there is insufficient evidence to justify the case being committed to the Crown Court. When section 44 of the Criminal Justice and Public Order Act 1994 comes into force, committal proceedings will be abolished, but it will still be possible for a defendant to make an application to the court for dismissal of the charges.

8.64   We have considered whether these procedures are a sufficient safeguard against the risk of private prosecutions for the corporate offence in cases where the CPS's decision not to prosecute is entirely justified. The effect of our proposed offence would be to make it easier to secure a conviction against a company whose operations have caused a death. It might therefore be argued that, if the evidence would be less likely to be held insufficient, it must also be less likely that proceedings would be brought on insufficient evidence. Moreover, the incidence of vexatious proceedings for manslaughter does not at present seem to be unduly high. However, this may be largely a consequence of the financial risk involved in bringing private proceedings that may result in an acquittal and an order for costs; the easier the offence is to prove, the smaller that risk will be perceived to be, and the more likely it is that private proceedings will be brought. And a proportion of those proceedings will undoubtedly be in cases that are clearly inappropriate for prosecution, even under the less restrictive rules that we propose.

8.65   We are aware that the definition of the offence we propose is in broad terms and relies to an unusual degree on the judgment of the jury. There will therefore be many cases where, although a jury would be *unlikely* to convict, it cannot be said that no reasonable jury *could* convict. In these cases the courts would have no power to prevent a private prosecution from going ahead (unless the proceedings appeared to be an abuse of the process of the court, which would be unlikely if there were a prima facie case), and it would be up to the CPS to intervene and discontinue the pro-

---

[106]   Code for Crown Prosecutors (June 1994) para 5.1.

[107]   As in the case of the sinking of the pleasure cruiser *Marchioness* on the River Thames on 20 August 1989, where judicial review was sought (without success) of the DPP's decision to charge only an offence under s 32 of the Merchant Shipping Act 1988 against the master of the *Bowbelle*. An application for judicial review would succeed only in limited circumstances, for example, where the DPP was shown to have acted in bad faith or to have failed to apply the Code for Crown Prosecutors (as in *R v DPP, ex p C* [1995] 1 Cr App R 136).

[108]   In *R v Bow Street Stipendiary Magistrate, ex p South Coast Shipping Co Ltd* (1993) 96 Cr App R 405 it was held that the DPP's decision not to bring manslaughter charges in respect of the *Marchioness* disaster (n 87 above) did not preclude the bringing of a private prosecution, subject to the right of the DPP to intervene in the proceedings and discontinue them.

[109]   Prosecution of Offences Act 1985, ss 6(2), 23.

[110]   *Turner v DPP* (1979) 68 Cr App R 70.

ceedings on the ground that there is no "realistic prospect of a conviction"—in other words, that an acquittal is a more likely outcome than a conviction. In such a case the CPS will not begin or continue a prosecution: the question whether the public interest requires a prosecution does not arise.

8.66   However, the right of a private individual to bring criminal proceedings, subject to the usual controls, is in our view an important one which should not be lightly set aside. Indeed, in a sense it is precisely the kind of case with which we are here concerned, where the public pressure for a prosecution is likely to be at its greatest, that that right is most important: it is in the most serious cases, such as homicide, that a decision not to prosecute is most likely to be challenged. It would in our view be perverse to remove the right to bring a private prosecution in the very case where it is most likely to be invoked. **We recommend that there should be no requirement of consent to the bringing of private prosecutions for the corporate offence. (Recommendation 17)**

MODE OF TRIAL

8.67   Where a death has occurred, and is alleged to have been caused by conduct which not only fell below an acceptable standard but fell *far* below it, we do not believe it would ever be appropriate for the case to be heard by a magistrates' court. It is true that magistrates' courts often hear cases arising out of fatal accidents which are prosecuted under regulatory legislation such as the Health and Safety at Work etc Act 1974; but in these cases the causing of death is not part of the offence. As we have said before, the corporate offence is intended to be the corporate counterpart of the individual offence of killing by gross carelessness. The fact that it would be punishable only with a fine, and not with imprisonment, is attributable to our proposal that it should be capable of commission only by a corporation, and not to any difference in the perceived gravity of the two offences. **We recommend that the offence of corporate killing should be triable only on indictment. (Recommendation 18)**

ALTERNATIVE VERDICTS

8.68   In practice, there will commonly be an overlap between the proposed new offence and the offences under sections 2 and 3 of the Health and Safety at Work etc Act 1974, which impose a duty on an employer to conduct her undertaking in such a way as to ensure, so far as reasonably practicable, that others are not thereby exposed to risks to their health and safety.[111] There may well be cases where a corporation is acquitted of the corporate offence but has no defence to a charge under one of these sections, and in such a case we think it should be open to the jury to convict of an offence under the appropriate section. It would clearly be inconvenient if, whenever preferring an indictment for the corporate offence, the prosecution had to choose between including a count of an offence under the 1974 Act and abandoning the chance of a conviction under that Act in the event of an acquittal of the corporate offence. On the other hand it is doubtful whether an alternative verdict under the 1974 Act would be available by virtue of section 6(3) of the Criminal Law Act 1967, which applies only where "the allegations in the indictment amount to or include (expressly or by implication) an allegation of another offence".[112] We think it should be made clear that on a charge of the corporate offence the jury has power to convict the corporation, instead, of one or other of these offences under the 1974

---

[111]   The Court of Appeal, in one important "policy" decision, *British Steel plc* [1995] ICR 586, a case which happened to involve a fatal accident, has held that the identification doctrine does not apply to these offences; and that, in effect, a corporation is vicariously liable for the conduct of all its employees. See paras 6.18–6.22 [...].

[112]   See para 5.57 n 93 [...].

Act.[113] This would of course be subject to the control of the judge: if, in the light of the evidence and the way the trial has been conducted, it would be in any way unfair to the defendant to leave the alternative to the jury, the judge will not do so.

8.69   We also think that it should be possible for the jury to convict of either of these offences on a count charging one of the *individual* offences we propose. There are two reasons for this, one somewhat theoretical and one practical. The theoretical reason is that we do not propose that corporations should be immune from prosecution for the individual offences, subject to the ordinary rules governing liability under the existing principle of identification. It is conceivable, though unlikely, that if our recommendations were implemented a corporation might be charged with reckless killing, or killing by gross carelessness, and not with the corporate offence. In such a case we see no reason why an alternative verdict under the 1974 Act should not be available.

8.70   The practical reason is that a charge of the corporate offence may well be tried together with a charge of killing by gross carelessness (or reckless killing) against one or more of the company's directors or managers. If the company were guilty of an offence under section 2 or 3 of the 1974 Act, those individuals might also be guilty of that offence.[114] It would be anomalous if there were power to return an alternative verdict against the company but not against its controllers, where they are facing what is for practical purposes the same charge. **We therefore recommend that, where the jury finds a defendant not guilty of any of the offences we recommend, it should be possible (subject to the overall discretion of the judge) for the jury to convict the defendant of an offence under section 2 of 3 of the Health and Safety at Work etc Act 1974. (Recommendation 19)**

THE COURT'S POWERS ON CONVICTION

Compensation

8.71   The court would have its ordinary powers to order compensation.[115]

Remedial action

8.72   On conviction of a corporation of an offence under the 1974 Act, the court has power to order the cause of the offence to be remedied (in addition to, or instead of, imposing punishment).[116] We did not raise this issue in Consultation Paper No 135, but in their responses on consultation some respondents who favoured an extension of corporate liability said that they contemplated that the court would have power not only to fine but also to order the taking of remedial action.[117]

---

[113]   Section 2 is confined to employees of the defendant corporation, s 3 to others.

[114]   s 37(1); see para 8.56 above.

[115]   See para 7.25 [...].

[116]   Health and Safety at Work etc Act 1974, s 42. Section 42(1) provides that where a person is convicted of an offence under the relevant statutory provisions in respect of any matters which appear to the court to be matters which it is in his power to remedy, the court may, in addition to or instead of imposing any punishment, order him, within such time as may be fixed by the order, to take such steps as may be specified in the order for remedying the said matters. The other four subsections of s 42 contain ancillary provisions, including a power to extend time for compliance with the order on an application before the end of the time originally fixed, and also a power to order the forfeiture and destruction of an explosive acquired, possessed or used in contravention of the Act.

[117]   See paras 7.15–7.16 [...].

8.73   We believe that in the interests of future safety it would be useful for the court to have such a power. Because the failure which will lead to a conviction is a management failure it is, we believe, necessary to make it clear that the court's remedial powers will extend to requiring the corporation to remedy any matter which appears to the court to have resulted from the failure and been the cause or one of the causes of the death.

8.74   This will be a quite novel power in the context of a conviction for a serious criminal offence in the Crown Court, and we believe that it is necessary to include some provision to assist the judge in selecting the type of order she might make.[118] In an ordinary case of sentencing an individual, the judge will be able to rely not only on her own sentencing experience but also, in cases of any difficulty, on a pre-sentence report. In the present context she will have no such experience on which to draw.

8.75   For this reason we think it desirable that there should be an onus on the prosecution[119] to apply for a remedial order, if it considers the case warrants the making of such an order, and to specify the terms of the order it proposes. It should then be open to the prosecution and the convicted corporation to adduce evidence and to make representations to the judge, by analogy with the present statutory procedure for making compensation orders.[120] The court should then have power to make such an order, if any, as it considers appropriate in the circumstances. An appeal against such an order would then lie to the Court of Appeal (Criminal Division) in the usual way.[121]

8.76   For these reasons **we recommend that**

(1) **a court before which a corporation is convicted of corporate killing should have power to order the corporation to take such steps, within such time, as the order specifies for remedying the failure in question and any matter which appears to the court to have resulted from the failure and been the cause or one of the causes of the death;[122]**

(2) **the power to make such an order should arise only on an application by the prosecution (or the Health and Safety Executive or any other body or person designated for this purpose by the Secretary of State, either generally or in relation to the case in question)[123]** specifying the terms of the proposed order;[124] and

(3) **any such order should be on such terms (whether those proposed or others) as the court considers appropriate having regard to any representations made, and any evidence adduced, by the prosecution (or any other body or person**

---

[118]   By analogy with the court's power to make a mandatory injunction in civil proceedings, where the party seeking the injunction will place before the court a draft of the order she seeks.
[119]   Because some other investigating agency may have been responsible for investigating the causes of the death or deaths, we recommend that this term should include the Health and Safety Executive and any other body or person designated for this purpose by the Secretary of State either generally or in relation to the case in question.
[120]   See Powers of Criminal Courts Act 1973 s 35(1A), as inserted by Criminal Justice Act 1982 s 67.
[121]   See Criminal Appeal Act 1968 s 50(1), where a sentence is defined to include "any order made by a court when dealing with an offender". See also *Hayden* (1974) 60 Cr App R 304 for the principle that a court order dependent on conviction falls within the definition of the word "sentence" in the 1968 Act.
[122]   See cl 5(1) of the draft Bill in Appendix A.
[123]   See cl 5(3) of the draft Bill.
[124]   See cl 5(2) of the draft Bill.

applying for such an order) or on behalf of the corporation.[125] (Recommendation 20)

CORPORATE LIABILITY FOR THE INDIVIDUAL OFFENCES

8.77   We recommended above[126] that there should be no question of *individual* liability for the *corporate* offence, because that offence is intended as a practical device to ensure that corporations cannot escape liability for killing by gross carelessness merely because their decision-making structures are large and complex. It does not follow, in our view, that there should be no *corporate* liability for the offences we have (for convenience) referred to as the *individual* offences. The existence of the corporate offence would normally make it unnecessary for the prosecution to charge a corporation with reckless killing or killing by gross carelessness, and thus undertake the burden of showing that a "controlling mind" of the corporation was guilty of the offence charged: even if no such person could be identified, the corporation could still be convicted of a homicide offence if the death were caused by a management failure of the requisite gravity. But, just because it would not normally be *necessary* to charge the corporation with an individual offence, it does not follow that it would never be *appropriate*; still less does it follow that it should not be *possible*. There may be the occasional case where, although under the identification principle the conduct of the individual responsible is the conduct of the company, it is arguable that that conduct does not amount to a *management* failure. Even where this is not the case, on facts such as those of the Lyme Bay tragedy[127] we see no reason why it should not continue to be possible for the company to be convicted of the same offence as the individual responsible. **We recommend that the ordinary principles of corporate liability should apply to the individual offences that we propose. (Recommendation 21)**

---

[125]   *Ibid.*

[126]   Paras 8.56–8.58.

[127]   *Kite and OLL Ltd*; see para 6.48 [...].

IOD

INSTITUTE OF DIRECTORS
and
HEALTH AND SAFETY COMMISSION

HSC

leading
health
and safety
at work

1 plan
2 deliver
3 monitor
4 review

**LEADERSHIP
ACTIONS FOR
DIRECTORS AND
BOARD MEMBERS**

www.iod.com/hsguide
www.hse.gov.uk/leadership

" Board level involvement is an essential part of the 21st century trading ethic. Attitudes to health and safety are determined by the bosses, not the organisation's size. "

" Health and safety is integral to success. Board members who do not show leadership in this area are failing in their duty as directors and their moral duty, and are damaging their organisation. "

" An organisation will never be able to achieve the highest standards of health and safety management without the active involvement of directors. External stakeholders viewing the organisation will observe the lack of direction. "

" Health and safety is a fundamental part of business. Boards need someone with passion and energy to ensure it stays at the core of the organisation. "

Quotes from health and safety leaders in the public and private sectors.

The Institute of Directors and the Health and Safety Commission would like to thank the following organisations for their help on the steering group that developed this guidance: Confederation of British Industry, Federation of Small Businesses, Institution of Occupational Safety and Health, Local Authorities Coordinators of Regulatory Services, Local Government Association, National Council for Voluntary Organisations, NHS Confederation, The Princess Alice Hospice, Trades Union Congress, University of Warwick.

introduction

This guidance sets out an agenda for the effective leadership of health and safety. It is designed for use by all directors, governors, trustees, officers and their equivalents in the private, public and third sectors. It applies to organisations of all sizes.*

Protecting the health and safety of employees or members of the public who may be affected by your activities is an essential part of risk management and must be led by the board.

Failure to include health and safety as a key business risk in board decisions can have catastrophic results. Many high-profile safety cases over the years have been rooted in failures of leadership.

Health and safety law places duties on organisations and employers, and directors can be personally liable when these duties are breached: members of the board have both collective and individual responsibility for health and safety.

By following this guidance, you will help your organisation find the best ways to lead and promote health and safety, and therefore meet its legal obligations.

The starting points are the following essential principles. These principles are intended to underpin the actions in this guidance and so lead to good health and safety performance.

ESSENTIAL PRINCIPLES

- Strong and active leadership from the top:
  - visible, active commitment from the board;
  - establishing effective 'downward' communication systems and management structures;
  - integration of good health and safety management with business decisions.

- Worker involvement:
  - engaging the workforce in the promotion and achievement of safe and healthy conditions;
  - effective 'upward' communication;
  - providing high quality training.

- Assessment and review:
  - identifying and managing health and safety risks;
  - accessing (and following) competent advice;
  - monitoring, reporting and reviewing performance.

*The Health and Safety Executive (HSE) has further advice on leadership for small businesses and major hazard industries – see resources section.

Costs of poor health and safety at work

HSE statistics reveal the human and financial cost of failing to address health and safety.

- More than 200 people are killed at work in the United Kingdom each year. This does not include work-related road deaths.
- In 2006, 30 million working days were lost in the UK to occupational ill health and injury, imposing an annual cost to society of £30 bn (more than 3% of GDP).
- Surveys show that about two million people suffer from an illness that they believe to be caused or made worse by work.
- Many thousands of deaths each year can be attributed to occupational illnesses, including some cancers and respiratory diseases.

Organisations can incur further costs – such as uninsured losses and loss of reputation.

IN THIS GUIDANCE

The following pages set out:

- a four-point agenda for embedding the essential health and safety principles;

- a summary of legal liabilities;

- a checklist of key questions;

- a list of resources and references for implementing this guidance in detail.

The agenda consists of:

Core actions for boards and individual board members that relate directly to the legal duties of an organisation. *These actions are intended to set a standard.*

Good practice guidelines that set out ways to give the core actions practical effect. *These guidelines provide ideas on how you might achieve the core actions.*

Case studies selected to be relevant to most sectors.

A website, www.hse.gov.uk/leadership, provides links to all the resources mentioned.

Benefits of good health and safety

Addressing health and safety should not be seen as a regulatory burden: it offers significant opportunities. Benefits can include:

- reduced costs and reduced risks – employee absence and turnover rates are lower, accidents are fewer, the threat of legal action is lessened;

- improved standing among suppliers and partners;

- a better reputation for corporate responsibility among investors, customers and communities;

- increased productivity – employees are healthier, happier and better motivated.

It includes online and downloadable versions of this guidance and further advice for small enterprises.

Legal responsibilities of employers

Health and safety law states that organisations must:

- provide a written health and safety policy (if they employ five or more people);

- assess risks to employees, customers, partners and any other people who could be affected by their activities;

- arrange for the effective planning, organisation, control, monitoring and review of preventive and protective measures;

- ensure they have access to competent health and safety advice;

- consult employees about their risks at work and current preventive and protective measures.

Failure to comply with these requirements can have serious consequences – for both organisations and individuals. Sanctions include fines, imprisonment and disqualification.

Under the Corporate Manslaughter and Corporate Homicide Act 2007 an offence will be committed where failings by an organisation's senior management are a substantial element in any gross breach of the duty of care owed to the organisation's employees or members of the public, which results in death. The maximum penalty is an unlimited fine and the court can additionally make a publicity order requiring the organisation to publish details of its conviction and fine. (See also the back page of this guidance.)

plan the direction for health and safety

The board should set the direction for effective health and safety management. Board members need to establish a health and safety policy that is much more than a document – it should be an integral part of your organisation's culture, of its values and performance standards.

All board members should take the lead in ensuring the communication of health and safety duties and benefits throughout the organisation. Executive directors must develop policies to avoid health and safety problems and must respond quickly where difficulties arise or new risks are introduced; non-executives must make sure that health and safety is properly addressed.

CORE ACTIONS

To agree a policy, boards will need to ensure they are aware of the significant risks faced by their organisation.

The policy should set out the board's own role and that of individual board members in leading the health and safety of its organisation. It should require the board to:

- 'own' and understand the key issues involved;

- decide how best to communicate, promote and champion health and safety.

The health and safety policy is a 'living' document and it should evolve over time, eg in the light of major organisational changes such as restructuring or a significant acquisition.

GOOD PRACTICE

- Health and safety should appear regularly on the agenda for board meetings.

- The chief executive can give the clearest visibility of leadership, but some boards find it useful to name one of their number as the health and safety 'champion'.

- The presence on the board of a health and safety director can be a strong signal that the issue is being taken seriously and that its **strategic importance** is understood.

- Setting targets helps define what the board is seeking to achieve.

- A non-executive director can act as a scrutineer – ensuring the processes to support boards facing significant health and safety risks are robust.

Corporate governance

For many organisations, health and safety is a corporate governance issue. The board should integrate health and safety into the main governance structures, including board sub-committees, such as risk, remuneration and audit.

The Turnbull guidance on the Combined Code on Corporate Governance requires listed companies to have robust systems of internal control, covering not just 'narrow' financial risks but also risks relating to the environment, business reputation and health and safety.

Case study – North Staffordshire Combined Healthcare NHS Trust

The board found itself facing service improvement targets. Using new corporate and clinical guidance, it set about taking a 'whole systems' approach to managing corporate risk, giving one of its directors responsibility for the leadership of health and safety for the first time. Health and safety was also made a key item on the board agenda.

This has resulted in a much better integrated health and safety management system that increases the opportunity to identify and manage all corporate risks, and a much more open culture, improving reporting and monitoring. The board actively promotes a culture that gives staff the confidence to report incidents. This has resulted in:
- 16% reduction in incidence rates over two years;
- 10% reduction in insurance premiums.

deliver
health and safety

Delivery depends on an effective management system to ensure, so far as is reasonably practicable, the health and safety of employees, customers and members of the public.

Organisations should aim to protect people by introducing management systems and practices that ensure risks are dealt with sensibly, responsibly and proportionately.

CORE ACTIONS

To take responsibility and 'ownership' of health and safety, members of the board must ensure that:

- health and safety arrangements are adequately resourced;
- they obtain competent health and safety advice;
- risk assessments are carried out;
- employees or their representatives are involved in decisions that affect their health and safety.

The board should consider the health and safety implications of introducing new processes, new working practices or new personnel, dedicating adequate resources to the task and seeking advice where necessary.

Boardroom decisions must be made in the context of the organisation's health and safety policy; it is important to 'design-in' health and safety when implementing change.

GOOD PRACTICE

- Leadership is more effective if visible – board members can reinforce health and safety policy by being seen on the 'shop floor', following all safety measures themselves and addressing any breaches immediately.
- Consider health and safety when deciding senior management appointments.
- Having procurement standards for goods, equipment and services can help prevent the introduction of expensive health and safety hazards.
- The health and safety arrangements of partners, key suppliers and contractors should be assessed: their performance could adversely affect yours.
- Setting up a separate risk management or health and safety committee as a subset of the board, chaired by a senior executive, can make sure the key issues are addressed and guard against time and effort being wasted on trivial risks and unnecessary bureaucracy.
- Providing health and safety training to some or all of the board can promote understanding and knowledge of the key issues in your organisation.
- Supporting worker involvement in health and safety, above your legal duty to consult worker representatives, can improve participation and help prove your commitment.

Case study – British Sugar

British Sugar was devastated in 2003, when three workers died. The business had always considered health and safety a key priority but realised a change in focus was needed. It carried out a comprehensive, boardroom-led review of its arrangements. This included:

- the chief executive assigning health and safety responsibilities to all directors;
- monthly reports on health and safety going to the board;
- more effective working partnerships with employees, trade unions and others;
- overseeing an audited behavioural change programme;
- publishing annual health and safety targets and initiatives to meet them.

Results included:

- 43% drop in time lost to injuries over two years;
- 63% reduction in major health and safety issues in one year;
- much greater understanding among directors of health and safety risks.

monitor
health and safety

Monitoring and reporting are vital parts of a health and safety culture. Management systems must allow the board to receive both specific (eg incident-led) and routine reports on the performance of health and safety policy.

Much day-to-day health and safety information need be reported only at the time of a formal review (see action 4). But only a strong system of monitoring can ensure that the formal review can proceed as planned – and that relevant events in the interim are brought to the board's attention.

CORE ACTIONS

The board should ensure that:

 appropriate weight is given to reporting both preventive information (such as progress of training and maintenance programmes) and incident data (such as accident and sickness absence rates);

■ periodic audits of the effectiveness of management structures and risk controls for health and safety are carried out;

■ the impact of changes such as the introduction of new procedures, work processes or products, or any major health and safety failure, is reported as soon as possible to the board;

■ there are procedures to implement new and changed legal requirements and to consider other external developments and events.

GOOD PRACTICE

■ Effective monitoring of sickness absence and workplace health can alert the board to underlying problems that could seriously damage performance or result in accidents and long-term illness.

■ The collection of workplace health and safety data can allow the board to benchmark the organisation's performance against others in its sector.

■ Appraisals of senior managers can include an assessment of their contribution to health and safety performance.

■ Boards can receive regular reports on the health and safety performance and actions of contractors.

■ Some organisations have found they win greater support for health and safety by involving workers in monitoring.

Case study – Mid and West Wales Fire and Rescue Service

Mid and West Wales Fire and Rescue Service recognised that it was critical to demonstrate to staff that health and safety was fundamental to the success of its overall service delivery – and that commitment to health and safety came from the top of the organisation. The director of service policy and planning was made health and safety director, and implemented a revised framework for health and safety. The director made site visits to engage the workforce and placed renewed emphasis on the need to improve incident reporting, investigation and monitoring procedures. The service has reported:

■ £100 000 reduction in insurance liability premiums in one year through improved corporate strategic risk management;

■ 50% reduction in sickness absence resulting from work-related injury over two years;

■ 50% reduction in injury rates over three years.

review
health and safety

A formal boardroom review of health and safety performance is essential. It allows the board to establish whether the essential health and safety principles – strong and active leadership, worker involvement, and assessment and review – have been embedded in the organisation. It tells you whether your system is effective in managing risk and protecting people.

CORE ACTIONS

The board should review health and safety performance at least once a year. The review process should:

☑ examine whether the health and safety policy reflects the organisation's current priorities, plans and targets;

☑ examine whether risk management and other health and safety structures have been effectively reporting to the board;

☑ report health and safety shortcomings, and the effect of all relevant board and management decisions;

☑ decide actions to address any weaknesses and a system to monitor their implementation;

☑ consider immediate reviews in the light of major shortcomings or events.

GOOD PRACTICE

☑ Performance on health and safety and wellbeing is increasingly being recorded in organisations' annual reports to investors and stakeholders.

☑ Board members can make extra 'shop floor' visits to gather information for the formal review.

☑ Good health and safety performance can be celebrated at central and local level.

Auditing and reporting

Larger public and private sector organisations need to have formal procedures for auditing and reporting health and safety performance. The board should ensure that any audit is perceived as a positive management and boardroom tool. It should have unrestricted access to both external and internal auditors, keeping their cost-effectiveness, independence and objectivity under review.

Various codes and guides (many of them sector-specific) are available to help organisations report health and safety performance and risk management as part of good governance. See resources section.

Case study – Sainsbury's

Sainsbury's rethought its approach to health and safety after an external audit highlighted the need for a more unified approach across the company. The key element was a health and safety vision, set out by the group HR director and backed by a plan that included targets over three years.

As part of the plan, all board directors were given training on health and safety responsibilities. Health and safety now regularly features on board agendas.

The business benefits include:

■ 17% reduction in sickness absence;

■ 28% reduction in reportable incidents;

■ improved morale and pride in working for the company, as indicated by colleague surveys.

when leadership
falls short

When board members do not lead effectively on health and safety management the consequences can be severe. These examples mark issues for all boards to consider.

Competent advice, training and supervision

Following the fatal injury of an employee maintaining machinery at a recycling firm employing approximately 30 people, a company director received a 12-month custodial sentence for manslaughter. The machinery was not properly isolated and started up unexpectedly. An HSE and police investigation revealed there was no safe system of work for maintenance; instruction, training and supervision were inadequate. HSE's investigating principal inspector said: 'Evidence showed that the director chose not to follow the advice of his health and safety advisor and instead adopted a complacent attitude, allowing the standards in his business to fall.'

Monitoring

The managing director of a manufacturing company with around 100 workers was sentenced to 12 months' imprisonment for manslaughter following the death of an employee who became caught in unguarded machinery. The investigation revealed that, had the company adequately maintained guarding around a conveyor, the death would have been avoided. The judge made clear that whether the managing director was aware of the situation was not the issue: he should have known as this was a long-standing problem. An area manager also received a custodial sentence. The company received a substantial fine and had to pay the prosecution's costs.

Risk assessment

A company and its officers were fined a total of £245 000 and ordered to pay costs of £75 500 at Crown Court in relation to the removal of asbestos. The company employed ten, mostly young, temporary workers; they were not trained or equipped to safely remove the asbestos, nor warned of its risk. The directors were also disqualified from holding any company directorship for two years and one year respectively.

Legal liability of individual board members for health and safety failures

If a health and safety offence is committed with the consent or connivance of, or is attributable to any neglect on the part of, any director, manager, secretary or other similar officer of the organisation, then that person (as well as the organisation) can be prosecuted under section 37 of the Health and Safety at Work etc Act 1974.

Recent case law has confirmed that directors cannot avoid a charge of neglect under section 37 by arranging their organisation's business so as to leave them ignorant of circumstances which would trigger their obligation to address health and safety breaches.

Those found guilty are liable for fines and, in some cases, imprisonment. In addition, the Company Directors Disqualification Act 1986, section 2(1), empowers the court to disqualify an individual convicted of an offence in connection with the management of a company. This includes health and safety offences. This power is exercised at the discretion of the court; it requires no additional investigation or evidence.

Individual directors are also potentially liable for other related offences, such as the common law offence of gross negligence manslaughter. Under the common law, gross negligence manslaughter is proved when individual officers of a company (directors or business owners) by their own grossly negligent behaviour cause death. This offence is punishable by a maximum of life imprisonment.

Note: equivalent legislation exists in Northern Ireland, ie article 34A of the Health and Safety at Work (Northern Ireland) Order 1978 and article 3(1) of the Company Directors Disqualification (Northern Ireland) Order 2002.

health and safety
leadership checklist

This list is designed to check your status as a *leader* on health and safety. See the resources section for advice and tools that may help you answer these questions.

- ☑ How do you demonstrate the board's commitment to health and safety?

- ☑ What do you do to ensure appropriate board-level review of health and safety?

- ☑ What have you done to ensure your organisation, at all levels including the board, receives competent health and safety advice?

- ☑ How are you ensuring all staff – including the board – are sufficiently trained and competent in their health and safety responsibilities?

- ☑ How confident are you that your workforce, particularly safety representatives, are consulted properly on health and safety matters, and that their concerns are reaching the appropriate level including, as necessary, the board?

- ☑ What systems are in place to ensure your organisation's risks are assessed, and that sensible control measures are established and maintained?

- ☑ How well do you know what is happening on the ground, and what audits or assessments are undertaken to inform you about what your organisation and contractors actually do?

- ☑ What information does the board receive regularly about health and safety, eg performance data and reports on injuries and work-related ill health?

- ☑ What targets have you set to improve health and safety and do you benchmark your performance against others in your sector or beyond?

- ☑ Where changes in working arrangements have significant implications for health and safety, how are these brought to the attention of the board?

key resources

A dedicated web page has been created to provide boards and board members with further advice and guidance. It includes links to various publications and websites, as well as online and downloadable versions of this guidance.

The web page can be found at: www.hse.gov.uk/leadership

You can get further information from the following organisations:

Health and Safety Executive (HSE) (www.hse.gov.uk)
- *Successful health and safety management* HSG65 HSE Books 1997 ISBN 978 0 7176 1276 5
- *Leadership for the major hazard industries* Leaflet INDG277(rev1) www.hse.gov.uk/pubns/indg277.pdf
- small businesses
- principles of sensible risk management
- measuring health and safety performance
- competent health and safety assistance
- worker involvement
- case studies and tools
- enforcement

Health and Safety Executive for Northern Ireland (www.hseni.gov.uk)

Institute of Directors (IoD) (www.iod.com)
- dedicated web page at: www.iod.com/hsguide
- *Wellbeing at work: A Director's Guide* IoD 2006 ISBN 978 1 9045 2048 1

Institution of Occupational Safety and Health (IOSH) (www.iosh.co.uk)
- *Questioning performance: The director's essential guide to health, safety and the environment* IOSH ISBN 978 0 901357 37 3
- toolkits
- competent health and safety assistance

Royal Society for the Prevention of Accidents (RoSPA) (www.rospa.com)
- DASH: Director Action on Safety and Health
- GoPoP: Going Public on Performance – measuring and reporting on health and safety performance
- case studies

Trades Union Congress (TUC) (www.tuc.org.uk)
- safety representatives

Business Link (www.businesslink.gov.uk)
- managing health and safety

European Agency for Safety and Health at Work (www.osha.europa.eu)

ABOUT THIS GUIDANCE

This guidance, issued jointly by the Institute of Directors and the Health and Safety Commission, is addressed to directors (and their equivalents) of corporate bodies and of organisations in the public and third sectors. Such organisations are required to comply with health and safety law. Although reference is made to existing legal obligations, following the guidance is not in itself obligatory. However, if you do follow it you will normally be doing enough to help your organisation meet its legal obligations.

In considering the liability of an organisation under the Corporate Manslaughter and Corporate Homicide Act 2007, a jury must consider any breaches of health and safety legislation and may have regard to any health and safety guidance. In addition to other health and safety guidance, this guidance could be a relevant consideration for a jury depending on the circumstances of the particular case.

FURTHER INFORMATION

HSE priced and free publications are available by mail order from HSE Books, PO Box 1999, Sudbury, Suffolk CO10 2WA Tel: 01787 881165 Fax: 01787 313995 Website: www.hsebooks.co.uk (HSE priced publications are also available from bookshops and free leaflets can be downloaded from HSE's website: www.hse.gov.uk.)

For information about health and safety ring HSE's Infoline Tel: 0845 345 0055 Fax: 0845 408 9566 Textphone: 0845 408 9577 e-mail: hse.infoline@natbrit.com or write to HSE Information Services, Caerphilly Business Park, Caerphilly CF83 3GG.

This leaflet is available in priced packs of 5 from HSE Books, ISBN 978 0 7176 6267 8. Single free copies are also available from HSE Books.

© *Crown copyright* This publication may be freely reproduced, except for advertising, endorsement or commercial purposes. First published 10/07. Please acknowledge the source as HSE.

INDG417   10/07   C2000
Printed and published by the Health and Safety Executive

APPENDIX 4

Extract from the Sentencing Advisory Panel,
Consultation Paper on Sentencing for Corporate Manslaughter,
November 15, 2007

B: THE OFFENCES

8. Section 1 of the CMA states that:
(1) An organisation to which this section applies is guilty of an offence if the way in which its activities are managed or organised—
(a) causes a person's death, and
(b) amounts to a gross breach of a relevant duty of care owed by the organisation to the deceased.

The legislation applies to all corporations and some unincorporated bodies such as trades unions, partnerships, employers' organisations and police forces. It also applies to most Crown bodies, although the CMA precludes a 'relevant duty of care' arising in respect of many of their activities.[128]

9. A gross breach is defined as conduct which falls far below what can reasonably be expected in the circumstances.[129] An organisation will only be guilty of the offence if the way in which its activities are managed or organised by its senior managers is a substantial element of the breach.[130] This test of 'senior management failure' was intended to ensure a wider application of the offence than was achieved under the common law, but it is not clear to what extent it broadens the requirement for a 'directing mind' into an aggregation of the conduct of a group of managers.

10. In deciding whether or not there was a gross breach the jury must consider whether the organisation failed to comply with relevant health and safety legislation and, if so, how serious that failure was and how much of a risk of death it posed.[131] The jury may also consider any relevant health and safety guidance and the extent to which the 'corporate culture' encouraged or produced tolerance of the health and safety breach.[132] These factors will also be relevant to the assessment of the seriousness of an offence for the purposes of sentencing.

11. The new offence is designed to complement rather than replace existing offences under the Health and Safety at Work etc Act 1974 (HSWA), the overarching leg-

---

[128] Activities excluded from the ambit of the offence include: public policy decisions; 'exclusively public functions'; certain military activities; policing and law enforcement; emergency service response; child protection and probation functions: ss.2-7. s.2(1) provides for a duty of care arising in respect of a person in custody, but the commencement of this section is subject to an affirmative resolution of both Houses of Parliament: s.27(2).
[129] CMA 2007, s.1(4)(b).
[130] ibid., s.1(3).
[131] ibid., s.8(2).
[132] ibid., s.8(3).

islation governing health and safety in the workplace in the United Kingdom.[133] Breaches of the HSWA or health and safety regulations are offences under section 33, punishable by an unlimited fine in the Crown Court. In a magistrates' court, breach of any of the general duties under sections 2 to 6 is punishable by a fine of up to £20,000; for most other offences, including breaches of health and safety regulations, the maximum fine is £5,000.

12. Most prosecutions of employers under the HSWA are based on breaches of the general duties set out in sections 2 and 3. Section 2 states that it shall be the duty of every employer to ensure, so far as is reasonably practicable, the health, safety and welfare at work of all his employees. Section 3 states that it shall be the duty of every employer to conduct his undertaking in such a way as to ensure, so far as is reasonably practicable, that persons not in his employment who may be affected thereby are not thereby exposed to risks to their health or safety. There is a significant overlap between these statutory duties and the 'duty of care' referred to by the CMA.[134] Unless otherwise specified, references to 'breach(es)' in this paper are intended to cover breaches of both types of duty.

C: SERIOUSNESS

13. The seriousness of an offence is determined by an assessment of the culpability of the offender and any actual, intended or foreseeable harm involved in the offence.[135] Whilst corporate manslaughter is triable only upon indictment, health and safety offences are triable either way, indicating the wider range of seriousness that may be involved. In relation to the offences considered in this paper, this range will be reflected in the level of culpability, as the harm involved (the death of one or more person(s)) is the same.

Culpability

14. The culpability of the offender should be the initial factor in determining the seriousness of any offence.[136] The critical factor will be the extent to which the conduct of the offender fell below the appropriate standard. A failure to keep pace with changing standards is likely to be one of the factors taken into account by the court. The degree of risk and the extent of danger will be relevant in assessing culpability, and it will be particularly significant whether the death was the result of an isolated breach of duty, several breaches occurring at around the same time, or breaches that took place over a period of time.[137]

15. Convictions for corporate manslaughter will always involve conduct that falls 'far below what can reasonably be expected of the organisation in the circumstances.' The offence of causing death by dangerous driving involves a similar standard of liability,[138] being 'driving that falls far below what would be expected of a competent and careful driver'. The grading of offences covered in this paper and the issues arising from them bear many similarities to the death by driving offences on which the Panel has recently consulted.

---

[133] *Corporate Manslaughter: The Government's Draft Bill for Reform*, para. 5; see fn. 7.
[134] For more detail on this point and commentary on the CMA as a whole see *A guide to the Corporate Manslaughter and Corporate Homicide Act 2007* (October 2007), Ministry of Justice; www.justice.gov.uk/docs/guidetomanslaughterhomicide07.pdf.
[135] Criminal Justice Act 2003, s.143.
[136] SGC Guideline, *Overarching Principles: Seriousness* (2004); www.sentencing-guidelines.gov.uk.
[137] *Howe and Son (Engineers) Ltd* [1999] 2 Cr App R (S) 37; *Balfour Beatty Rail Infra-structure Services Ltd* [2007] Cr App R (S).
[138] Road Traffic Act 1988, s.2A. See also the joint Parliamentary Select Committee report on the Draft Corporate Manslaughter Bill (HC 540 2005-06), para. 174.

16. Breaches of the duties under sections 2 and 3 HSWA involve failure to take all 'reasonably practicable' steps to ensure the safety of employees and/or the public. Therefore they will encompass a wider range of culpability than offences of corporate manslaughter, up to and possibly overlapping with the latter. For example, an offence under the HSWA may involve conduct falling far below the standard expected but the test of 'senior management failure'[139] may not be satisfied.

Harm

17. An offence of corporate manslaughter or a breach of the HSWA resulting in death involves actual harm of the highest level: the death of one or more person. These offences generally will not involve any intention to cause harm, but in most cases harm (if not death) will have been foreseeable. The extent of the risk of death posed by any breach of health and safety legislation is a factor the jury must consider when deciding whether an offence of corporate manslaughter has been committed. The extent of foreseeable harm involved in the offence will also be relevant to the assessment of seriousness for the purposes of sentencing.

Aggravating and mitigating factors

18. In light of the above paragraphs, there are a small number of particular factors that may aggravate or mitigate the seriousness of an offence of the type covered in this paper.[140] The proposals for sentencing set out later in this paper relate to a first time offender pleading not guilty. However, where there is a guilty plea to an offence under the HSWA it is now common practice for the prosecution to serve a 'Friskies schedule',[141] setting out the aggravating and mitigating features of the case for agreement with the defendant.

Aggravating factors affecting the level of harm
More than one person killed as a result of the offence
19. In *Balfour Beatty*, the Court stated that an offence under the HSWA involving more than one death must be regarded as more serious, by analogy with cases of causing death by dangerous driving.[142] It is clear that the level of harm is higher where more than one death has resulted. However, whilst some breaches obviously produce a risk of harm to a large number of people, in others the number of deaths likely to result is not so obvious. Offences will be most serious where a number of deaths occur *and* that would reasonably have been foreseeable as a result of the breach.

Serious injury caused to one or more others, in addition to the death(s)
20. As well as the death caused by the breach, there may be serious injury caused to other people. Indeed, it is often a matter of chance whether or not injuries are so severe as to result in death. It is clear that such injuries increase the harm caused by the offence and so increase the seriousness of the offence whether under the CMA or HSWA.

Aggravating factors affecting the degree of culpability
Failure to act upon advice, cautions or warning from regulatory authorities
21. If the offending organisation was warned of the inadequacies of its safety standards by the regulatory authorities but took no action before the death(s) occurred,

---

[139] See para. 6 [...].
[140] See Annex C for the Council's list of general aggravating and mitigating factors.
[141] The schedule has come to be known by this name since the decision in *Friskies Petcare Ltd* [2000] Cr App R (S) 401, when the Court of Appeal recommended that the defence and prosecution should set out these features in advance.
[142] This factor and the others referred to as aggravating an offence of causing death by dangerous driving would aggravate any 'death by driving' offence.

this will clearly increase culpability.[143] In 1997, for example, inspectors from the HSE had spoken to English Brothers Ltd construction company about a gang foreman working without the correct safety equipment. Nothing was done to improve the situation, and two years later the same employee fell though a fragile roof to his death. The company pleaded guilty to manslaughter under the common law[144] and was fined £25,000.[145]

22. As the HSE notes in relation to sentencing for health and safety offences,[146] other warnings to which an organisation should have responded may include previous incidents of a similar nature. In 2001 the London Borough of Hammersmith and Fulham was fined £350,000 for offences under the HSWA, following the death of two council tenants from carbon monoxide poisoning as a result of a faulty boiler that was overdue its annual safety check. The sentencing judge condemned the offender for 'prolonged dereliction of duty', noting that an earlier death in the same circumstances "provided the plainest salutary lesson imaginable", which regrettably had not been learned.[147]

Failure to heed relevant concerns of employees or others
23. Specific warnings may originate from sources other than the authorities and, if unheeded, also may increase culpability and so aggravate the seriousness of an offence where it is apparent that action should have been taken. The first company to be convicted of manslaughter under the common law was OLL Ltd, which operated an activity centre in Lyme Regis. In 1992 two instructors resigned in protest at poor safety standards, one warning the managing director in writing that lives might be endangered if standards were not improved. A year later four school pupils drowned during a canoeing trip. The company was fined £60,000 and the director was sentenced to three years imprisonment, reduced to two years on appeal.[148]

Offender carrying out operations without an appropriate licence
24. Licensing systems exist to help ensure safety in the workplace for employees and other members of the public. Organisations working with hazardous substances such as asbestos or explosives, or in a hazardous industry such as construction or diving, are generally required to hold a relevant licence. Operating without a required licence will usually constitute a separate offence, but will also increase culpability in relation to an offence of corporate manslaughter and/or an offence under the HSWA involving death.

Action or lack of action prompted by financial or other inappropriate motives
25. If the appropriate standard of care has been breached deliberately with a view to profit, this will be a seriously aggravating feature.[149] For example, in 2004 Keymark Services haulage company pleaded guilty to common law manslaughter after one of its lorry drivers fell asleep on the motorway and collided with seven vehicles, killing himself and two other drivers. The subsequent investigation revealed that employees regularly tampered with tachographs and falsified records in order to work grossly excessive hours. This conduct appeared to be financially motivated.[150] The company was fined a total of £50,000 for both manslaughter and health and safety offences; the

---

[143] *Howe*; see fn. 20.
[144] See para. 5 [...].
[145] www.corporateaccountability.org.
[146] www.hse.gov.uk/enforce/enforcementguide/court/sentencing/factors.htm#P3_586.
[147] Gerard Forlin and Michael Appleby, *Corporate Liability: Work Related Deaths and Criminal Prosecutions* (2003).
[148] *Kite* [1996] 2 Cr App R (S) 295.
[149] *Howe, Balfour Beatty*; see fn. 20.
[150] news.bbc.co.uk/1/hi/england/4066331.stm.

managing director was sentenced to 7 years imprisonment.[151] This is one of the longest sentences imposed for the common law offence,[152] reflecting the gravity of risking death in order to profit financially.

26. Organisations such as charities and public bodies do not make profits, but might still deliberately compromise safety standards.

Corporate culture encouraging or producing tolerance of breach of duty

27. Under the CMA, factors that the jury may consider when deciding whether a gross breach has been committed include whether there were attitudes, policies, systems or accepted practices within the organisation that were likely to have encouraged or produced tolerance of the relevant failure.[153] These were found to aggravate the offences of manslaughter committed by Keymark Services (see above), where every driver employed by the company was found to have been involved in falsifying records. The sentencing judge is reported to have described the scale of the offence(s) as "shocking", saying it was "hard to imagine a more serious case of its type".[154]

Mitigating factors
Breach due to employee acting outside authority or failing in duties

28. The immediate cause of many safety-related incidents involving organisations is employee behaviour rather than failure of systems or equipment. However, the HSE is of the view that such incidents usually stem from organisational failures which are the responsibility of management, and an offence under the HSWA will be made out if the organisation did not take all reasonably practical steps to avoid safety risks, through measures such as the training and supervision of employees.[155] An employer will not have a defence to a health and safety prosecution because of any act or default by an employee.[156] Nevertheless, if the failure of an employee has been a contributory factor it may be considered appropriate for this to mitigate the seriousness of an offence under the HSWA involving death.

29. The requirement under the CMA for senior management failure to be a substantial cause of the breach is designed to exclude liability of an organisation for "immediate, operational negligence causing death or indeed for the unpredictable, maverick acts of its employees."[157] If a death has resulted from the actions of a maverick employee acting outside authority, in most cases the offence of corporate manslaughter will not be made out. However, there may be convictions under the CMA where the immediate failure of an employee (whether or not the person who died) also contributed to the offence. In such a case the court will take the contributory conduct into consideration, but the fact that the offence involves a gross breach of the relevant duty of care suggests that any impact on sentence will be limited.

---

[151] www.northants.police.uk/extranet2/default.asp?action = article&ID = 6633.

[152] Following the Tebay rail deaths in 2004 the owner and operator of the machinery company responsible was sentenced to 9 years, reduced to 7 on appeal: *Connolly* [2007] EWCA Crim 790. The jury found that the defendant had deliberately disabled the braking system and then concealed the disablement. The motive for this conduct was said by Holland J to be "solely profit", and this was the first aggravating factor mentioned by the judge when sentencing the defendant at first instance.

[153] CMA 2007, s.8(3).

[154] See fn. 33 [...].

[155] *Successful health and safety management*, HSE (1997).

[156] Management of Health and Safety at Work Regulations 1999 (SI 1999/3242), reg. 21.

[157] *Corporate Manslaughter: The Government's Draft Bill for Reform*, para. 26; see fn. 7.

Offender mitigation
Ready cooperation with authorities
30. Ready cooperation with the relevant authorities and steps taken to remedy safety failures as soon as possible after the offence will constitute general offender mitigation. However, it should be noted that a court is likely to give credit only where the offender has initiated remedial action of its own volition rather than under pressure from the enforcement authorities.

Good previous safety record
31. One of the mitigating factors listed in *Howe* and endorsed in *Balfour Beatty* is a good safety record. An excellent record might be considered relevant for some offences under the HSWA involving death, but there may be few (if any) cases where an organisation in gross breach of its duty of care would have such a record or, even if it did, where it should have a significant effect on sentence.

Summary
32. The primary factor in assessing the seriousness of an offence of corporate manslaughter or of an HSWA offence that has resulted in death is the extent to which the conduct of the offender fell below the appropriate standard of care. The following aggravating or mitigating factors are relevant:

Aggravating factors increasing the level of harm

- more than one person killed
- serious injury to one or more person(s)

Aggravating factors affecting the degree of culpability

- failure to act upon advice, cautions or warning from regulatory authorities
- failure to heed relevant concerns of employees or others
- carrying out operations without an appropriate licence
- financial or other inappropriate motive
- corporate culture encouraging or producing tolerance of breach of duty

Mitigating factor

- employee acting outside authority or failing in duties

Offender mitigation

- ready co-operation with authorities
- good safety record

Question 1
Do you agree with the approach to the assessment of seriousness?

Question 2
Is each of the above aggravating and mitigating factors relevant to sentencing for a) an offence of corporate manslaughter and b) an offence under the HSWA involving death? Are there are any other factors which may aggravate or mitigate either or both of these types of offence?

D: AIMS OF SENTENCING

33. There are three sanctions available to the court when sentencing for the new offence of corporate manslaughter: unlimited fine, publicity order and remedial order. Under the HSWA only an unlimited fine and a remedial order are available;[158] the court has no power to make a publicity order, although the HSE website contains a public database of organisations convicted under the Act since 2000, which has become known as the 'name and shame' list.[159]

34. The offence of corporate manslaughter is intended to reflect the gravity of the most serious instances of management failure resulting in death.[160] The joint Parliamentary Select Committee report on the Draft Corporate Manslaughter Bill viewed the seriousness of the offence as equivalent to that of causing death by dangerous driving, and proposed the same maximum sentence (14 years imprisonment) if the offence were to apply to an individual.[161] As mentioned above, the courts have imposed substantial prison sentences on company directors found guilty of the common law offence of manslaughter by gross negligence. The CMA applies only to organisations and, therefore, imprisonment is not an option, but it is important that the sanctions that *are* available reflect adequately the perception of seriousness of the offence.

35. As well as enabling the punishment of organisations in such circumstances, the possibility of a conviction for the new offence is expected to provide an extra deterrent against unsafe working practices.[162] General and individual deterrence are also important aims of prosecutions for regulatory offences under the HSWA, which is designed to protect employees and the wider public. In contrast to individual offenders,[163] it is widely agreed that deterrent sentencing can be effective for corporate offenders.[164]

36. The availability of a range of sanctions thus enables a court to further four of the purposes of sentencing set out in the Criminal Justice Act (CJA) 2003: punishment of offenders and reduction of crime through the punitive and deterrent effects of fines and publicity orders, reform and rehabilitation of offenders through remedial orders, and the protection of the public through both deterrence and remedial action. The fifth aim of reparation by offenders to those affected by the offence can be addressed by a remedial order or a compensation order, which are discussed further below.[165]
37. These aims may be of varying importance depending on whether the sentence is imposed for an offence of corporate manslaughter or an offence under the HSWA involving death. For example, punishment may be considered to be more relevant when deciding the most appropriate sentence for corporate manslaughter as it will involve a higher level of culpability at senior management level.[166]

---

[158] Under s.42, where it appears to the court that it is in the offender's power to remedy any matters in respect of the offence, the court can (in addition to or instead of any other sentence) order the offender to take steps to remedy those matters.
[159] Gerard Forlin and Michael Appleby, *Corporate Liability: Work Related Deaths and Criminal Prosecutions* (2003).
[160] *Corporate Manslaughter: The Government's Draft Bill for Reform*, para. 32; see fn. 7.
[161] Para. 314; see fn. 21.
[162] *Corporate Manslaughter: The Government's Draft Bill for Reform*, para. 6.
[163] See e.g. Halliday report *Making Punishments Work: Report of a Review of the Sentencing Framework for England and Wales*, Home Office (2001), which reviewed the evidence for the deterrent effects of sentencing individuals.
[164] Hazel Croall, *Penalties for Corporate Homicide*, published as Annex B to *Corporate Homicide: Expert Group Report*, Scottish Executive (2005); www.scotland.gov.uk/Resource/Doc/76169/0019246.pdf.
[165] Paras. 84-89 below.
[166] See para. 9 above.

38. When sentencing for either type of offence, the court will be alert to the possibility of conflict between these aims. For example, a fine set at a high level to punish the offender may make it difficult for the organisation to invest in improved health and safety practices that prevent further offending and protect the public. A publicity order that leads to loss of business may exacerbate this situation by indirectly reducing the resources of the organisation still further.

Question 3
What do you consider should be the main aim of sentencing an organisation for an offence of corporate manslaughter or an offence under the HSWA involving death? Should there be any difference between the two types of offence and, if so, why?

E: THE SANCTIONS AVAILABLE AND THE PANEL'S PROPOSALS

Fines
39. The maximum fine is unlimited for offences under the CMA, as it is for offences under the HSWA when sentenced in the Crown Court. The basic approach to fixing any fine is the same whether the offender is an organisation or an individual. The amount of the fine must reflect the seriousness of the offence[167] and the court must take into account the financial circumstances of the offender.[168] The information about financial circumstances may have the effect of either increasing or decreasing the amount of the fine.[169] Considerations that may arise where the offender is a publicly funded body are discussed below.[170]

Current practice
40. Fines imposed on organisations for offences of manslaughter by gross negligence and for offences under the HSWA involving death have been criticised as being too low in relation to the harm and culpability concerned.[171] The information available on current practice is very limited: the CMA is not yet in force, and the recording of sentences under the common law does not distinguish manslaughter by gross negligence from other types of manslaughter. The HSE provides some data on fines imposed following work-related fatalities, but this does not distinguish between individual offenders and organisations.

41. The fines imposed in cases of corporate manslaughter under the common law of which we are aware have ranged from £4,000 to £90,000 (the latter also including fines for health and safety offences). It should be noted that the offenders were all small companies, as the identification principle referred to above[172] has effectively prevented convictions of larger organisations.

42. When discussing health and safety offences in *Colthrop Board Mills Ltd*[173] the Court stated: "it appears from the authorities that financial penalties of up to around half a million pounds are appropriate for cases which result in the death even of a single employee." The Court was considering a review of reported HSWA cases made in the judgment of *Friskies Petcare (UK) Ltd*,[174] which had concluded that "fines in excess of £500,000...tend to be reserved for those cases where a major public disaster occurs." Leaving aside the exceptional cases mentioned below, fines

---

[167] CJA 2003, s.164(2).
[168] CJA 2003, s.164(3).
[169] CJA 2003, s.164(4).
[170] See paras. 71-74.
[171] In *Howe*, for example, the Court acknowledged that fines were too low for health and safety offences in general; see fn. 20.
[172] See para. 5.
[173] [2002] EWCA Crim 520 (a health and safety case that did not involve death).
[174] [2000] 2 Cr App R (S).

for corporate offences under HSWA involving death appear to range from £15,000 to £750,000.[175] When both corporate and individual convictions are taken into account, the average fine imposed following work-related fatalities in the UK in 2004/05 was £29,867.[176]

43. Over the last decade, high-profile health and safety cases involving multiple deaths have resulted in increasingly high fines. Great Western Trains was fined £1.5 million following the 1997 Southall train crash in which seven people died and 150 were injured. The train collision at Ladbroke Grove in which 31 people died and over 400 were injured in 1999 resulted in fines of £2 million for Thames Trains and £4 million for Network Rail.[177] Following the Hatfield train derailment in 2000, in which four people died and 102 were injured, Network Rail was fined £3.5 million and maintenance firm Balfour Beatty was fined £7.5 million.[178]

Aims of the fine
Reflecting serious concern at the loss of life
44. The Court stated in *Howe* that the fine should "reflect public disquiet at the unnecessary loss of life" where a death has occurred, although it is not possible to incorporate a financial measure of the value of human life in the fine imposed for an offence.[179] In the *Balfour Beatty* judgment the Court said that the fine must reflect both the degree of fault and the consequences of the breach so as to raise appropriate concern on the part of any shareholders. It was asserted that such an approach would ensure that the sentence serves the aims of both punishment and deterrence.

Ensuring future compliance with safety standards
45. In *Balfour Beatty* the Court also endorsed the statement in *Howe* that the ultimate objective of a fine for a health and safety offence in the workplace is to achieve a safe environment for employees and the public, through encouraging compliance with the offender's legal duties. The Court stated in *Howe* that the fine for an offence under the HSWA involving death needs to be large enough to "bring that message home" to those responsible for the governance of the organisation, not only managers but also any shareholders who may be able to influence company policy and practice. It was noted that, as well as deterring an individual organisation from future breaches of its duties, such a fine may provide a deterrent to other organisations.

46. The approach to the aim of a fine outlined above may also be appropriate for offences of corporate manslaughter. However, as an offence under the CMA will involve a *gross* breach of an organisation's duty of care, this will indicate higher culpability than that involved in many offences under the HSWA involving death and, therefore, a greater degree of seriousness. Moreover, 'bringing the message [of safety] home' to an organisation is a broad aim which the courts will bear in mind throughout the sentencing process rather than an approach which assists in the actual calculation of the fine.

---

[175] Gerard Forlin and Michael Appleby, *Corporate Liability: Work Related Deaths and Criminal Prosecutions* (2003).

[176] *Health and Safety Offences and Penalties 2004/05*, HSE; www.hse.gov.uk.

[177] Formerly Railtrack.

[178] This was originally £10 million but was reduced upon appeal: *Balfour Beatty Rail Infrastructure Services Ltd* [2007] Cr App R (S).

[179] *Friskies Petcare Ltd* [2000] Cr App R (S).

Eliminating financial benefit

47. A more specific approach has been suggested as providing an individual and general deterrent from offending. The recent Macrory review of regulatory penalties[180] recommended that these should aim to eliminate any financial gain or benefit resulting from non-compliance with safety standards. If the expected penalty cost does not outweigh the expected gain from the offence, an organisation might choose to take the risk of being detected and prosecuted.

48. The Panel has previously stated that, in principle, it should not be cheaper to offend than to prevent the commission of an offence.[181] However, whilst eliminating any financial benefit from the offence is a desirable aim, it is unlikely to be achievable in all circumstances. A court should request details of any gain made from the offence if such information is available, but it is not clear how profits made or costs that have been avoided, deferred or saved would be calculated. In some circumstances, a remedial order may be the most appropriate way to deal with this issue, indirectly eliminating financial benefit by compelling the offender to invest in bringing safety systems up to the appropriate standard.

49. In summary, the aims of the fine described above require that the amount should be sufficient:
a) to reflect serious concern at the consequences of the breach;
b) to ensure that those responsible for governance of the organisation are properly aware of the need to ensure a safe environment; and
c) if possible, to eliminate any financial benefit from the offence.
In fulfilling this aim, the court is obliged to have regard to both the seriousness of the offence and the financial circumstances of the offender.

Question 4
Do you agree that the aims of the fine should be to ensure future safety and reflect serious concern at the unnecessary loss of life? Should there be any difference in aim when imposing a fine for corporate manslaughter or for an offence under the HSWA involving death?

Question 5
Do you agree that a fine imposed for an offence of corporate manslaughter or an offence under the HSWA involving death should aim to eliminate any financial benefit resulting from the offence? If so, what information would be necessary, and how could this be obtained?

Methods of calculation
50. The comments made in the cases cited in paragraph 42 above indicate the desire for a consistent method of calculating the fine to reflect the seriousness of the offence and the financial circumstances of the offender. A lack of consistency in fines imposed was found by the Macrory review to be a major concern of bodies such as the HSE.[182] In 2004/05, for example, the average penalty following all HSE prosecutions in England was £20,647, while in Wales it was £8,189.[183] However, consistency of *approach* rather than *outcome* (i.e. quantum) is the aim, as the organisation's ability to pay must be taken into account. The Panel has considered a number of methods that could be used to develop a consistent approach to the setting of financial penalties for the offences covered in this paper.

---

[180] Richard Macrory, *Regulatory Justice: Making Sanctions Effective* (2006); www.cabinetoffice.gov.uk/regulation/reviewing_regulation/penalties/index.asp.
[181] Sentencing Advisory Panel, Advice on *Environmental Offences* (2000), para.16; www.sentencing-guidelines.gov.uk.
[182] See fn. 63 [...].
[183] *Health and Safety Offences and Penalties 2004/05*, HSE; www.hse.gov.uk.

Appendix 4

Optimal Penalties Model

51. This controversial approach for sentencing corporate offenders is based on the premise mentioned above,[184] that organisations that breach their legal duties do so on the basis of a calculation that the expected benefits of offending outweigh the expected costs. Under this model a court bases the amount of the fine on both the 'value' of all harm caused by the offence and the probability of conviction, often expressed as the multiplier of the chances of punishment; the total fine is equal to the harm divided by the probability of punishment. Both of these calculations present considerable practical challenges, and this model (which has been rejected both by the United States Federal Sentencing Commission and the Law Reform Commission of New South Wales) can result in fines that are no less arbitrary than penalties determined by a less complicated approach.

US Federal Sentencing Commission organisational guidelines

52. The model adopted by the US Federal Sentencing Commission in its organisational sentencing guidelines involves:

a) determining a base fine, which is the greater of: the guidelines-prescribed minimum for the offence; any caused intentionally, knowingly or recklessly;

b) multiplying the base fine by a 'culpability score,' which takes into account the following aggravating and mitigating factors: the level of authority of the employees involved; size of the organisation; any previous convictions; breaches of court orders; the presence of an effective programme to prevent breaches of the law; and whether the organisation cooperated with or obstructed the authorities.

The fine may be reduced if it is likely to impair the organisation's ability to make restitution or jeopardise the existence of the organisation.

53. The Law Reform Commission of New South Wales reviewed the US model and concluded that it adheres to the traditional sentencing principles of proportionality and deterrence.[185] There is some evidence that the guidelines have resulted in higher fines and lower levels of corporate offending.[186] However, as presently constructed they leave little room for judicial discretion and can arguably lead to undue rigidity, reasons given by the Law Reform Commission for rejecting such an approach to sentencing organisations.

54. Nevertheless, it may be possible to utilise the principles to assist in constructing sentencing ranges and starting points. The Panel has considered the pecuniary gain to the offender as mentioned in point a) above, and has asked consultees how this could be eliminated. The aggravating and mitigating factors listed in b) have been taken into account in the discussion of seriousness above, with the exception of the size of the organisation.

Fine expressed as percentage of turnover or profits

55. The size of the organisation is primarily relevant in terms of the financial resources available to the offender with which to pay the fine. As a general principle the Panel has previously stated that fines should be devised to have an equal economic impact on organisations of different sizes.[187] Such an approach would require an agreed method of calculation to determine an organisation's ability to pay. The

---

[184] See para. 47.
[185] *Sentencing: Corporate Offenders*, Report 102 (2003); www.agd.nsw.gov.au.
[186] Hazel Croall, *Penalties for Corporate Homicide*; see fn. 47.
[187] Sentencing Advisory Panel, Advice on *Environmental Offences* (2000), para. 22.

principal measures by which this ability can be assessed are turnover, profitability and liquidity.

56. In 1994, the Criminal Bar Association suggested that the maximum penalty for a proposed offence of corporate killing should be the greater of either a percentage of average profit in the 3 years preceding the offence or a percentage of turnover during the same period (tentatively 50 and 5 per cent respectively).[188] In 2005 the joint Parliamentary Select Committee report on the Draft Corporate Manslaughter Bill noted that many of their consultees had suggested 10 per cent of annual turnover as an appropriate fine for the new offence.[189]

57. Turnover is the aggregate of all sums of money received by an organisation during the course of its business (whether a private company, charity or public body) over an annual period. It compares closely with the income of an individual, which is typically the primary measure used to assess an individual offender's ability to pay a fine. It is also the measure already used by the Office of Fair Trading (OFT) when imposing financial penalties on companies that have infringed competition law. The OFT calculates the starting point with regard to a) the seriousness of the infringement and b) the company's turnover in the product market and geographic market affected by the infringement in the last business year.[190] Aggravating and mitigating factors such as the duration of the infringement are then taken into account, but in any event the fine must not exceed ten per cent of the company's worldwide turnover. Ten per cent of global turnover is also the maximum fine the European Commission can impose for breaches of European Community competition law.[191]

The Panel's proposals
58. The Panel's provisional view is that annual turnover is the most appropriate measure of an organisation's ability to pay a fine, and thus the starting points and ranges[192] proposed below are expressed as percentages of annual turnover. It would be for the prosecution to provide evidence of particularly high profitability if it considered the fine indicated by annual turnover to be too low, or for the offender to provide evidence of low liquidity if it considered the fine indicated by annual turnover to be too high.

59. The statutory offence of corporate manslaughter has been created for the most serious instances of management failure resulting in death. The Panel's view is that a fine imposed for an offence under the CMA should be set at a level significantly higher than for an offence under the HSWA involving death.[193] The fine levels proposed below for offences of corporate manslaughter are based on the assumption that a publicity order will be imposed on the offender.

60. The Panel's provisional starting point for an offence of corporate manslaughter committed by a first time offender pleading not guilty[194] is a fine amounting to 5 per cent of the offender's average annual turnover during the three years prior to sentencing (see paragraph 64 below). The court will then take into account any

---

[188]   As cited by the Centre for Corporate Accountability: www.corporateaccountability.org/dl/SentCCAresponse.pdf.
[189]   Para. 264; see fn. 21.
[190]   *OFT's guidance as to the appropriate amount of a penalty* (2004); www.oft.gov.uk.
[191]   Regulation 1/2003; www.europa.eu.
[192]   See Annex B for explanations of 'starting point', 'range' and 'first time offender'.
[193]   This was also the view of many of the witnesses who gave evidence to the joint Select Committee's consultation on the Draft Bill: see para. 264 of the report cited at fn. 21.
[194]   For guidance on the appropriate discount to be made where the offender has entered a guilty plea, see the revised Council Guideline: *Reduction in Sentence for a Guilty Plea* (2007); www.sentencing-guidelines.gov.uk.

aggravating and/or mitigating factors as set out above,[195] arriving at a fine which will normally fall within a range of 2.5 to 10 per cent of average annual turnover. Significant aggravating factors or previous convictions may take the fine beyond the range. The court will then consider any mitigation related to the offender (rather than the offence), which may take the fine below the range.

61. The Panel's provisional starting point for an offence under the HSWA involving death is a fine amounting to 2.5 per cent of average annual turnover during the three years prior to the offence. The fine will normally fall within a range of 1 to 7.5 per cent of average annual turnover.

62. Where the offender is a very large organisation, the Panel's provisional approach would result in larger fines than have been imposed previously by the courts. The largest fine imposed to date for a health and safety offence in the UK was that of £15 million in the Scottish case of Transco, for breaches of regulations which led to the deaths of four members of the same family in a gas explosion. The fine represented 5 per cent of the company's after-tax profits and less than one per cent of annual turnover. Although in that instance the offender did respond appropriately to the incident, it has been suggested that the fine in itself could be easily absorbed and may not have provided an effective individual or general deterrent as described above.[196] A fine expressed as a percentage of average annual turnover is designed to have an equal economic impact on all sizes of organisation, in order to reflect the seriousness of the offence even where the offender has large financial resources.

63. Conversely, where the offender has a very low annual turnover, it is possible that the Panel's provisional approach would result in smaller fines than those currently imposed in some cases, at least for offences under the HSWA resulting in death. The apparent disparity in actual terms between fines imposed on very small and very large offenders is an inevitable result of an approach designed to have a consistently equal economic impact. However, it may be thought appropriate to set a minimum fine for corporate manslaughter or for offences under the HSWA involving death, in order to ensure that the harm involved in such offences is properly reflected in the sentence.

Question 6
Do you agree with the Panel's proposed starting points and ranges for a) offences of corporate manslaughter and b) offences under the HSWA involving death? If not, what alternative approach would you suggest for the fining of organisations for these offences?

Question 7
Do you agree that it is for the prosecution and defence to raise issues of profitability and liquidity? What impact should these factors have on the calculation of the fine?

Question 8
Do you consider that there should be a minimum fine for a) offences of corporate manslaughter and b) offences under the HSWA involving death? If so, what amount do you think would be appropriate?

Provision of financial information
64. It is common practice for an organisation to supply its accounts to the court in order to demonstrate its ability to pay a fine for an offence under the HSWA, as otherwise the court is entitled to assume that the organisation can pay any fine it

---

[195] These are summarised at para. 32.
[196] *Regulatory Justice: Making Sanctions Effective*, para. 1.23; see fn. 63.

chooses to impose.[197] Under the Panel's proposed approach an offender should be required to provide comprehensive accounts for a three-year period, to enable the court to make an accurate assessment of its financial status. This period will usually be the last three financial years, but the court should be alert to the possibility that the organisation may try to rearrange its finances in order to receive a lower fine, particularly where several years have passed between the offence and the imposition of sentence. Where three years or more have passed in the interim, the court may also wish to examine accounts from a period prior to the offence.

65. In *Howe* the Court recognised that it can be difficult to obtain 'timely and accurate' information about the offender's resources, and there have been suggestions that courts should receive a form of 'pre-sentence report' including such details. The Law Reform Commission of New South Wales recommended that, where necessary, the court should be able to request a professional assessment of an offender's finances from a relevant expert, paid for where appropriate by the offender itself.[198] The Commission received positive responses to this suggestion in its consultation,[199] and the joint Select Committee report on the Draft Corporate Manslaughter Bill stated that it would be useful for such a 'pre-sentence report' to be provided for each offender, despite the risk that this might increase the delays already associated with the conduct of these cases. The Panel considers such a report to be desirable in principle, but it is unclear how and by whom it would be provided.

Question 9
Do you consider that a report on each offender should be prepared for the court with full details of financial status? If so, how would this be provided?

Potential reasons for deviating from the proposed fine levels
The 'deterrence trap'
66. As mentioned above, a fine set at a high level may hinder other aims of sentencing—the prevention of offending and the protection of the public - by reducing the resources available to the organisation to invest in improved health and safety practices. This 'deterrence trap' is of particular relevance where the organisation has a very small profit margin and is therefore less able to absorb the impact of paying a large fine.

The 'spill-over' effect
67. Another concern associated with large fines is the potential 'spill-over' effect on third parties such as employees, customers, and shareholders. First, where the organisation has no choice but to reduce its staffing budget in order to pay the fine, wage levels will be affected and jobs will be threatened. In some cases the court may be willing to take this into account, particularly where individuals have also been convicted of offences and where the organisation has not, in fact, benefited from the conduct.[200]

68. Secondly, the organisation may consider it necessary to increase the price of its goods or services as a result of paying a large fine. Depending on the business environment in which the offending organisation operates, customers may have the option of taking their custom elsewhere. However, this choice would be severely limited if the offender was a rail company, for example. Where the organisation is a public body the issue of price rises will not generally arise, but a large fine may force it to reduce its services, which will have an adverse impact on users (see further

---

[197] *Howe*; see fn. 20.
[198] *Sentencing: Corporate Offenders*; see fn. 68.
[199] Hazel Croall, *Penalties for Corporate Homicide*; see fn. 47.
[200] New South Wales Law Reform Commission, *Sentencing: Corporate Offenders*, para. 6.11; see fn. 68.

below). In these circumstances, the court may contemplate a reduction in fine, although it should first consider whether spreading the payment of the fine would be a more appropriate course of action.

69. Thirdly, it has been argued that the imposition of large fines can unfairly penalise shareholders who may be remote from the actions leading to a death and who may have little power to affect day-to-day management. On the other hand, shareholders have voluntarily taken a risk by investing, may actually profit from offences, can have an impact on management decisions and thus should not be protected from the effect of those decisions.[201] The Panel's provisional view is that the court should not make any adjustment to the fine to take account of a possible impact on shareholders.

70. Finally, in *Howe* the Court stated that in general a fine for a health and safety offence should not be so large as to imperil the commercial survival of the organisation, but that there may be cases where the offender ought not to be in business. Whilst the court will not aim directly to shut down an organisation, it may be less concerned at this prospect where an organisation has committed the offence of corporate manslaughter. Moreover, the Court of Appeal has established that, where appropriate, payment of the fine can be spread over a number of years.[202]

Offenders providing public services
71. Particular issues arise when the offending organisation is a public body, or a private or hybrid body providing what is considered to be a public service. In *Jarvis*, a health and safety case which did not involve death, the Court considered itself entitled to take a more severe view of breaches where there is a "significant public element", particularly where public safety is entrusted to companies such as those maintaining the railways. However, the courts have also reduced fines where the funds needed to pay the fine would otherwise be spent on public safety, for example in the case of Railtrack following the Ladbroke Grove disaster.

72. Crown bodies such as Government Departments are not currently subject to statutory enforcement or prosecution under the HSWA;[203] instead of a fine the only sanction available is a 'Crown censure.' The CMA applies to most Crown bodies but, as it precludes a 'relevant duty of care' arising in respect of many of their activities, the scope for conviction is limited. Where the offending organisation is a Crown or other publicly funded body such as a local authority or hospital trust any fine imposed may be considered an inefficient recycling of money or worse, if public services suffer as a result. However, it is important that a body that has committed an offence under the CMA or the HSWA does not escape sanction.[204] The Government has stated that the courts are alert to the issue of diverting resources and are able to set fines accordingly.[205]

---

[201] Hazel Croall, *Penalties for Corporate Homicide*; see fn. 47.
[202] *Rollco Screw & Rivet Co Ltd* [1999] 2 Cr App R (S) 436. In that case the Court reduced the payment period from six years and five months to five years and seven months.
[203] The Government made a commitment in 2000 to remove Crown immunity: *Revitalising Health and Safety Strategy Statement*, DETR (2000); this document can be found at www.hse.gov.uk/revitalising/strategy.pdf.
[204] This was the view of a majority of those who responded to the Government's consultation on the Draft Corporate Manslaughter Bill and those who gave evidence to the joint Select Committee; see, respectively, the *Summary of Responses* at www.homeoffice.gov.uk/documents/cons-2005-corporate-manslaughter/draft-bill-responses-2005-cons, and fn. 22 [...].
[205] *Government Reply to the first Joint Report from the Home Affairs and Work and Pensions Committees 2005-06 HC 540* (2006) Cm 6755, para. 46.

73. Where an offence under the CMA or the HSWA has involved foreseeable harm to a large number of people, such as a group of train passengers, this will be reflected in the level of seriousness as discussed above.[206] Actual harm such as multiple fatalities and/or serious injury will aggravate the offence. The objectives of the fine as discussed above, to reflect public concern at the harm caused by the offence and to deter the offender from breaching its duties in the future, are just as important whether fining a public body or a private company.

74. In summary, the assessment of financial circumstances will seek to ensure that:
a) the fine is sufficient to have the required impact, in most cases without imperilling either the existence of the organisation or the funds necessary to remedy defective systems; and
b) where the offender is funded from the public purse, it is recognised that the fine will be paid with public money.

Question 10
Do you agree with the Panel's approach to the impact of the fine on the offender, its employees, customers and shareholders? If not, why not?

Question 11
Do you agree that the court should treat offenders consistently, whether or not they are publicly funded or providing a public service? If not, how do you think that considerations specific to public bodies should be reflected?

Publicity orders
75. However large current fines may be, concerns remain over the sufficiency of their impact on large companies. The CMA provides for a publicity order through which a court will be able to require an organisation convicted of corporate manslaughter to advertise the fact of its conviction, specified particulars of the offence, the amount of any fine imposed, and the terms of any remedial order that has been made. This is a new power in the UK,[207] although it is already available for various offences in Canada, the United States and Australia. The normal expectation is that a publicity order would be imposed alongside a fine but there is nothing to prevent a court making a stand-alone order.

76. A publicity order is considered to be an effective deterrent, potentially exceeding the effect of a fine, as it can impact upon the public reputation of an organisation through damage to consumer confidence, market share and equity value. The HSE's 'name and shame' database launched in 2000 serves a similar purpose in relation to health and safety offences, providing a public record of all successful prosecutions and the names of convicted companies. However, the courts are not involved in the HSE database and it is not considered further here.

77. Prior to imposing an order the court will be required to ascertain the views of the appropriate regulatory authority, and also to have regard to any representations made by the prosecution and defence. In practice, the wording of the order usually will be suggested to the court by the regulator or prosecution following consultation with the victim's family. The order must specify the period within which the advert is to be placed and the court may require the organisation to supply evidence of

---

[206] See para. 17.
[207] Similar provisions were available in the 19th century that allowed courts to order the publication of certain details of convicted offenders and their offence. For example, in cases where the offender adulterated bread, statute provided for the offender's name, abode and offence to be published in a local newspaper, the cost of publication being deducted from the fine also imposed: London Bread Act 1822, s.10; Bread Act 1836, s.8: New South Wales Law Reform Commission, *Sentencing: Corporate Offenders*; see fn. 68.

compliance with the order to any regulator it has consulted. Failure to comply with an order will be an offence punishable on indictment by an unlimited fine.

78. Given the guidance on the face of the CMA and the involvement of the regulator and/or prosecution, the Panel does not consider it necessary or appropriate to consult on the content of a publicity order. However, it may be helpful for the court to have guidance on *whether* an order should be made, the extent of the publicity, and what effect (if any) it should have on the overall sentence.

Whether an order should be made
79. The order is primarily intended as an additional deterrent designed to put offenders at a disadvantage in comparison with competitors who do not break the law. The Law Reform Commission of New South Wales has suggested[208] that publicity orders may lose their efficacy if they are imposed on every organisation convicted of any type of offence but identified the following situations in which they might be most useful:

- the court has reduced a fine due to the organisation's financial circumstances
- the organisation has a poor record of compliance with the law (a publicity order may increase the pressure on the organisation to comply)
- it is considered that the organisation's customers, creditors and/or share-holders should know about the conviction, or where news coverage is likely to be insufficient (although it might be argued that most cases of corporate manslaughter would attract publicity).

80. The potentially 'desensitising' effect on the public of a regular use of publicity orders may be of less relevance to cases of corporate manslaughter. If it does serve a deterrent purpose, an order might be considered appropriate in most cases where the offender is operating in a competitive market. The Panel's provisional view is that, in principle, a publicity order should be imposed on every offender convicted of corporate manslaughter. However, there may be cases where the making of an order may be less appropriate, for example where the offender is providing a local public service in relation to which the public cannot exercise choice.

Question 12
Do you agree that, when sentencing an organisation for an offence of corporate manslaughter, the court should impose a publicity order?

The extent of publicity
81. A court may order that the details of an offence are published in any 'specified manner', giving the court scope to ensure that the publicity reaches its intended audience. Options for the form of the order include:

- publication on television/radio and/or in a local/national/trade newspaper, including relevant broadcaster/newspaper websites;
- publication on the organisation's website and in its annual report, informing (potential) customers and those who might be interested in investing in the organisation;
- notice to shareholders; and
- letters to customers and/or suppliers of the organisation.

82. In light of the range of offenders, the Panel does not consider it sensible to seek to provide detailed guidance on the extent of publicity, but it may be possible to set some minimum standards. For example, if the offender is a local organisation, it might normally be appropriate to require publication in the local media; in the case

---

[208] *Sentencing: Corporate Offenders*; Report 102 (2003); see fn. 68.

of a large national organisation, publication in national media would be more effective. In both cases, a notice in all relevant trade journals should be required. Any shareholders should be notified in order that they may press for enhanced health and safety standards and publication should always be required in an annual report.

Question 13
What should the extent of the publicity be and how (if at all) will this differ between cases of corporate manslaughter?

Effect on overall sentence
83. The requirements of a publicity order will entail both direct and indirect costs for the offending organisation. The direct costs to the offender of placing the advertisement and notifying shareholders are likely to be relatively small and easy to calculate. The indirect costs in the form of loss of custom and/or investment are potentially much larger and more difficult to estimate. However, as the Panel's proposed starting point and range for the financial penalty are based on the premise that a publicity order will be imposed in every case of corporate manslaughter, the court should not need to give any further consideration to the effect of such an order on the overall sentence. As mentioned earlier in paragraph 59, where a publicity order is not imposed, the court should consider whether a higher fine would be appropriate.

Question 14
Do you agree that the making of a publicity order should not lead to a reduction in the level of fine imposed on an organisation for an offence of corporate manslaughter?

Remedial orders
84. Both the CMA and the HSWA provide for rehabilitation of the offender through a remedial order, setting out steps to be taken to ensure that the failures that led to the death are addressed. Failure to comply with an order under the CMA will be an offence punishable on indictment by an unlimited fine. The availability of this sanction has been widely welcomed, even though it is unlikely to be used often in practice. The similar order available for offences under the HSWA[209] is itself rarely used, as by the time an organisation is sentenced for an offence, the regulatory authorities are likely to have taken any appropriate action.

85. The remedial order will provide an additional safeguarding power for a limited number of cases where the offender has failed to respond to other interventions. Therefore the Panel does not consider it to be necessary to consult on the situations in which it would be appropriate for a court to impose either this order or the order available under the HSWA. As a remedial order will only be imposed after consultation with a relevant regulatory body and will be highly case-specific, the Panel also does not consider it necessary to consult on the content of such an order.

86. With regard to the effect on overall sentence, the Panel's provisional view is that the costs involved in complying with the remedial order should not lead to a corresponding decrease in any fine imposed for the same offence. The order is rehabilitative rather than punitive, and merely requires the offender to take steps to comply with the health and safety standards already required by law. Any reduction in the fine would reward unfairly the few organisations that have resisted compliance with those standards, and would lead to inequitable treatment of the majority of organisations that have taken remedial action before the point of sentence.

---

[209]   s.42.

Appendix 4

Question 15
Do you agree that the making of a remedial order should not lead to a reduction in the level of fine imposed on an organisation for an offence of corporate manslaughter or an offence under the HSWA involving death?

Compensation orders
87. The court has the power to make an order requiring the organisation to pay compensation for any personal injury, loss or damage resulting from the offence,[210] and must give reasons for its decision if it does not make such an order.[211] A compensation order can be made in favour of the relatives and dependants of the deceased, in respect of bereavement and funeral expenses.[212] An order in respect of funeral expenses can be made for the benefit of anyone who has incurred them,[213] but compensation for bereavement can only be made in favour of persons who could claim damages for bereavement under the Fatal Accidents Act 1976,[214] namely the spouse of the deceased or, in the case of a minor, his/her parents. The maximum sum which may be claimed for bereavement is £10,000.[215]

88. More than one person may have been killed as a result of the offence; others may have been injured. The amount of compensation should be such as the court considers appropriate, having regard to the offender's means. Where both a fine and a compensation order are appropriate but the offender lacks the means to pay both, the compensation order payments will take priority. Compensation paid is deducted from any damages received in civil proceedings, so the existence of a pending civil claim should not in itself prevent the imposition of a compensation order.

89. However, in cases prosecuted for the offences considered in this paper, the level of complexity surrounding the calculation of compensation is likely to be such that it is an issue best resolved outside the criminal proceedings. Whilst a court is always under an obligation to consider whether a compensation order can be made, it is more likely that a court will decide to leave the issue to the civil court, in which case it must give its reasons for doing so.

SUMMARY OF PROPOSALS

90. When sentencing for an offence of corporate manslaughter, the starting point should be:

- the imposition of a publicity order (see paragraphs 75-83); and
- a fine of 5 per cent of the offender's average annual turnover (see paragraph 60);
- within a fine range of 2.5 - 10 per cent of average annual turnover.

91. When sentencing for an offence under the HSWA involving death, the starting point should be:

- a fine of 2.5 per cent of the offender's average annual turnover (see paragraph 61);
- within a fine range of 1 - 7.5 per cent of average annual turnover.

---

[210] Powers of Criminal Courts (Sentencing) Act (PCCSA) 2000, s.130(1).
[211] s.130(4).
[212] PCCSA 2000, s.130(1)(b).
[213] s.130 (9).
[214] s.1A.
[215] Damages for Bereavement (Variation of Sum) (England and Wales) Order (SI 2002/644).

INDEX